Born to Serve

THE

EVOLUTION

OF THE SOUL

THROUGH SERVICE

Born to Serve

by Susan S. Trout, Ph.D.

WITH A FOREWORD BY HIS HOLINESS THE DALAI LAMA

THREE ROSES PRESS / ALEXANDRIA, VIRGINIA

Published by Three Roses Press, P. O. Box 19222, Alexandria, VA 22320

Printed in the United States of America

ISBN: 0-9625386-2-0
Library of Congress Catalog Card Number: 96-090760

Cover and text design by Jane Perini
Author photograph by Suly Uberman
Jacket illustration: detail, *Creation of Adam* (1511)
by Michelangelo Buonarroti, Sistine Chapel, Vatican City

to

Jehawa

CONTENTS

PART TWO

The Stages of Service

PART THREE

Unveiling the Soul

$\mathcal{F}$OREWORD

$\mathcal{B}$e wisely selfish and know that your happiness depends on the happiness of those around you and the world in general. If society suffers you will suffer, so love yourself enough to work for the social good.

–THE DALAI LAMA

*A*s human beings we all want to be happy. One of the most important foundations for happiness is mental peace. From my own limited experience I have found that the greatest inner tranquility comes from the development of love and compassion.

The more we care for the happiness of others, the greater is our own sense of well-being. Cultivating a close, warmhearted feeling for others automatically puts the mind at ease. It helps remove whatever fears or insecurities we may have and gives us the strength to cope with any obstacles we encounter. It is the ultimate source of happiness in life. If we remember that it is not just ourselves, but everyone who has to undergo suffering, this realistic perspective will increase our determination and capacity to overcome difficulties. Indeed, with this attitude, each new obstacle can be seen as another valuable opportunity to improve our minds.

Whether people are beautiful and friendly or unattractive and disruptive, ultimately they are human beings, just like ourselves. Like us, they want happiness and do not want suffering. Moreover, their right to overcome suffering and be happy is equal to our own. When we recognize that all beings are equal in both their desire for happiness and their right to obtain it, we automatically feel an empathy and closeness towards them. Through acquainting our minds with this sense of universal altruism, we develop a feeling of responsibility for others: the wish to help them actively overcome their problems. This wish is not selective; it applies equally to all. As long as there are human beings experiencing pleasure and pain, just as we do, there is no reason for discriminating between them by altering our concern for them if they behave negatively.

Recent advances in science and technology have led all over

When we recognize that all beings are equal in both their desire for happiness and their right to obtain it, we automatically feel an empathy and closeness towards them.

the world to an undue emphasis solely on material development. We have become so engrossed in its pursuit that, almost without knowing it, we have neglected to foster the most basic human needs for love, kindness, cooperation, and caring. But the development of human society is based entirely on people helping each other. If we lose this essential humanity, what is the point of pursuing only material improvement?

If we lose this essential humanity, what is the point of pursuing only material improvement?

In this book Dr. Susan Trout draws on her long experience to discuss serving others as a means to greater happiness and spiritual development. We find that this is one of the common elements of almost all spiritual traditions. Indeed, I believe it reflects a fundamental aspect of human nature. Because we all share a wish for happiness and an identical need for love, it is possible to feel that anybody we meet, in whatever circumstances, is a brother or sister. We do not need to become religious; nor do we need to believe in an ideology. However, at every level of society the key to a happier and more successful world is the growth of compassion and the active wish to help each other.

The Dalai Lama
Dharamsala, Himachal Pradesh, India
March 31, 1997

REFACE

In the process of my journey I have learned a very important lesson: being of service means doing whatever needs to be done with no attachment to the form of the task and with no investment in its outcome. I have also learned there is an integral relationship between service and my own personal healing process.

–SUSAN S. TROUT

*D*uring the thirty years of my friendship with Susan Trout, I have watched the journey of her life as directed by her driving desire to understand service. Underneath this drive, I think, runs an even deeper river: a calling to experience joy—that deep, in-the-bones, peace-of-mind experience of God in each moment. From my vantage point, service is her medium, joy her goal. To these two things she has applied a singleness of purpose I have rarely encountered in anyone else whose focus has been inner rather than outer.

In *Born to Serve*, Susan extends the enormous gift of her life's journey to individuals and organizations. This gift has the potential to transform the way our society views service during the next century. The proof of her contribution is manifested by those whom she has already taught through her work as Executive Director of the Insititute for Attitudinal Studies in Alexandria, Virginia, and through her very being. Those of her students who have integrated what is presented in this book have each become a pebble of service dropped in the water of life. In this way the ripples of Susan's work are already reaching around the world.

Through her background in psychoneurology and communication disorders Susan possesses an understanding of scientific inquiry and research. She applies this analytical approach to everything—her own life and work and the study of psychospiritual development and organizational systems. She then synthesizes her observations and study of the empirical with her deep inner spiritual experience. Finally and almost immediately, she is able to envision the practical application of this synthesis. This ability to swiftly move from study to theory to

This ability to swiftly move from study to theory to revelation to practice is the gift of Susan's cognitive and spiritual process.

revelation to practice is the gift of Susan's cognitive and spiritual process. *Born to Serve* is the result of just such an integration of sound psychological research, inner revelation, and years of observation and application.

Service is the mirror of our relationship with God, for we cannot love God any more than we love others; and we cannot love others any more than we love ourselves.

Born to Serve turns Western culture's current view of service upside down. It challenges individuals and organizations to view everything, all of life, as service. In this new definition, service is not limited to some—the poor, the disabled, the sick, the dying; it pervades every encounter and every action. Service is the mirror of our relationship with God, for we cannot love God any more than we love others; and we cannot love others any more than we love ourselves. This concept of service challenges the individual to accept responsibility for the sculpting of his or her own soul; it challenges religions to focus on the deepest and most mystical truths of their teachings; and it challenges the culture as a whole to shift from an outer directed search for happiness to an inner directed experience of peace.

In *Born to Serve*, Susan presents service (by which she means the giving and receiving involved in every encounter) as the context for the deep personal inner work necessary to unveil the perfection of the individual soul. Inner work is work with the shadow side of ourselves, that part of ourselves, positive and negative, that we disown and deny. In the context of service, the shadow consists of our hidden motivations for serving. Becoming aware of "why" we serve raises our consciousness and brings us closer to God. The process of self-discovery is developmental in nature. We can choose to participate in our own development by increasing our willingness to meet the shadow, to use the "blows" of our life experiences as the tools for removing the obstacles to the discovery of our innermost selves.

I believe this book is a classic. In the sixteenth century, St. Teresa of Avila wrote *The Interior Castle* in which she described stages of development of the soul. She wrote the book for the sisters of the order she founded, the Carmelites. She wrote in Christian terms for those leading a monastic life. The only purpose for seeking the inner room of the castle where God dwells, St. Teresa wrote, is to take what one experienced there out into the world to help others. St. Teresa saw service as the result of the search for the inner room.

I feel that *Born to Serve* is *The Interior Castle* for the twenty-first century. Susan wrote it for lay people who seek to make the spiritual practical in their daily lives. She wrote it from an inclusive point of view, transcending dogma and doctrine. Susan sees service as both the castle through which we engage in the search and the result of the search. As our search is refined, so is our service. *Born to Serve* provides a roadmap through the castle to the inner room in which we are reborn as mystics, as selfless servers, as One with the Unknowable Absolute. Nothing is required but our willingness to let go, to fall unencumbered. For most of us arriving at the jump site is the result of an arduous journey and the decision to jump the result of great inner conflict and struggle.

Only when we feel driven, usually by despair, to fill our yearning for wholeness, do we surrender to the understanding that who we are is not determined by what we do in the world, but rather by our state of being. We then see that there is a reciprocal, dynamic, and ever-deepening relationship between our process of healing ourselves and the depth and breadth of our service to others.

In *Born to Serve*, the reader is invited to plunge into the intensity of exploring service as a way to become free from the entanglements and attachments of personality and to live in har-

Born to Serve provides a roadmap through the castle to the inner room in which we are reborn as mystics, as selfless servers, as One with the Unknowable Absolute.

mony with the soul's true nature. Susan Trout leads the way on a path of service for all of us who know we were born to learn, to grow, and to serve.

Peggy Tabor Millin, M.A.
Asheville, NC
February 1997

PART ONE

Service and the Unfoldment of the Soul

A woman lay in a daisy field watching the clouds and contemplating her life. She remembered with deep regret all the times she had harmed herself and others. With all her heart, she looked to the heavens and asked for forgiveness.

Suddenly one of the clouds descended. Standing on it was an angel child who beckoned the woman to board the cloud. She did as bidden. The two rode the cloud to a great building in which there were many men, women, and children of all races, colors, creeds, and religions. The angel child led the woman inside where she was presented with a white book beautifully decorated with a gold rose. Then he led her back to the cloud and guided it back to the daisy field.

The woman had barely been able to contain her excitement over her gift. Alone in the field, she examined the book. When she opened it, she saw there was only one page. And on that page was written:

There is nothing to forgive.
Use what you have learned from your life to help others.

$\mathcal{I}$NTRODUCTION

$\mathcal{L}$ife, with its achievements and challenges, its joys and sorrows, gifts us with many opportunities to grow and serve. We serve when we willingly share the wisdom we have gleaned from our life experiences. The spirit of our life is made visible in the spirit of our giving and receiving.

Service pervades all of life. It is present in our communications with family, colleagues, and friends. The spirit of service exists in all activities of life, whether we cook meals, teach school, paint pictures, tend gardens, sweep streets, build buildings, or visit someone who is ill.

As we evolve spiritually, service is less about doing and more about being. We move from being outer directed to inner directed. More and more, we focus on the quality of our mind while living and working in the outer world.

Service is a dynamic partnership between the server and the served. We are all servers and we are all being served. The quality of our motivations, not the form of our service, determines the quality of our service.

STRUCTURE OF *BORN TO SERVE*

Following this introduction, the prologue entitled "Service as the Masterpiece of the Soul" captures the essence of *Born to Serve*. The book's intent is to bring clarity and inspiration to service as a medium we can use to consciously sculpt our souls and our lives as masterpieces.

The book is divided into three parts. Part One: Service and the Unfoldment of the Soul explores the nature of the soul and its relationship to service. It defines the role of service in spiritual traditions and addresses how our hidden motivations can impact the quality of our service. Part One serves as the psychological and spiritual framework for the seven evolutionary stages of service discussed in Part Two: The Stages of Service. Part Three: Unveiling the Soul contains suggestions for indepth study of the book and methods and exercises for identifying and working with the shadow of service.

STRUCTURE OF PART ONE

THE NATURE OF SERVICE

This chapter explores our soul's innate urge to serve and the role of personal choice in manifesting service in the world. A system of natural laws supports the soul's urge to service. Ten laws of service are identified and described—the laws of synchronicity, *dharma*, omnipresence, evolution, receiving, uniformity, extension, agreement, transmutation, and transcendence.

Exploration of the relationship of personal growth to service is essential to understanding the nature of service. The Universal Tributes are introduced in this chapter as guidelines for unifying the self and service and for actualizing the principle that giving and receiving are the same. The Tributes are discussed in detail in Part Two, Stage Five: Healing the Healer.

SERVICE AND THE EVOLUTION OF THE SOUL

Service is an expression of our soul's evolution. This chapter discusses the aspects of this evolution, including parameters of the soul's evolution, aspects of the soul's unfoldment, cycles of life, styles of service, and evolutionary shifts currently taking place in our consciousness of service. This chapter introduces the soul's seven evolutionary stages of service: Awakening to Serve, Work Ethic, Missionary Attitude, Wounded Healer, Healing the Healer, Selfless Action, and Beyond the Physical. These stages are discussed in depth in Part Two.

THE DIMENSIONS OF SERVICE

Service is an integral part of the world's five major religions. There are four spiritual dimensions to service: duty, charity, purification, and devotion. Duty is explored as giving, good works, a container for life, and spiritual practice. Service as charity is defined as the ability to give the right thing in the right amount at the right time and for the right reason. Service as purification allows service to be used as a means to clarify and purify hidden motivations. Viewing service as the altar of devotion is the purest form of service.

THE SHADOW OF SERVICE

Our motivations impact the quality of our service. Hidden motives reside in our shadow, an unconscious aspect of our psyche. Projection, denial, and neglect are shadow qualities that impact our service. Projections of the shadow become visible in power and fame, pride, sentiment, and attachment. The denied shadow appears as evasion of service and incompetence and the neglected shadow as avoidance of caring for our physical, mental, emotional, and spiritual health.

PROLOGUE

Service as the Masterpiece of the Soul

Beauteous art, brought with us from heaven,
will conquer nature; so divine a power
belongs to him who strives with every nerve.
If I was made for art, from childhood given
a prey for burning beauty to devour,
I blame the mistress I was born to serve.

—MICHELANGELO BUONARROTI

*A*s certainly as he revealed the soul of the marble he sculpted, Michelangelo's own soul was revealed through his partnership with the stone; this was how he served art and, through art, humanity. Like him, we reveal our souls through our service. We are always in partnership with that which we serve and are served by, whether people, animals, nature, or task. Serving with the intention of being both the master sculptor and the masterpiece of our lives opens the door for the Absolute to create the highest good in any given set of circumstances.

As a sculptor, Michelangelo saw in his mind's eye the figure within each massive piece of marble. His heart resonated with the potential sculpture that lived within the stone. The reciprocity between Michelangelo and the figure within was pure, vibrant, and certain. A sculptor cannot force a design on marble that does not agree with its nature. Rather, as he chiseled, burnished, and polished its surface, Michelangelo and the marble spoke and cooperated with one another until together they released the statue that revealed both the sculptor's and the marble's perfected potential. Michelangelo and the marble were one.

Michelangelo pounded and chiseled with force, concentration, and purposefulness until his vision, the "soul" of the marble, emerged from the stone. The marble yielded to Michelangelo's blows, not out of sacrifice but out of desire for the figure within to reveal itself. Through this mutual give and take, Michelangelo removed all obstacles to the marble's complete expression of itself, simultaneously becoming the complete expression of himself in that moment.

We are sculptors of our lives and can use each life experience to remove the superfluous in our inner and outer lives and thereby free the soul's knowledge, its already perfected potential. The

We are sculptors of our lives and can use each life experience to remove the superfluous in our inner and outer lives and thereby free the soul's knowledge, its already perfected potential.

emergence of spiritual knowledge is the destiny of the soul.

The outside forces of painful experiences serve as catalysts for inner change and transformation. As our personality tendencies and limited perceptions of life experience fall away, all our soul powers are called forth into full expression on the physical plane. In this process, we discover both our human psychology and our divine spirituality. The once hidden qualities and features of the soul emerge, and with increasing consciousness, we manifest them in the world through service.

Through service, we become equal partners joined in a common purpose rather than separated individuals doing something to one another.

To recognize and relate to another's fullest potential is to honor another's soul. Through service, we become equal partners joined in a common purpose rather than separated individuals doing something to one another. Sometimes we are the sculptor and sometimes the marble; sometimes we are the student, sometimes the teacher. Joined in this way, we release something far greater than is otherwise possible: a holy relationship in which we support the emergence of each other's highest potential into a joint masterpiece.

To release the soul to its full expression requires skills for working with the physical, psychological, and spiritual nature of ourselves and others. This is a lifelong process; this is the reason we are here. When our "striving with every nerve" joins with divine grace, the extraordinary happens. Our wills become one with Divine Will. We know what to say or do to sculpt our soul's unique masterpiece of service. Only by accepting the rigorous discipline of this partnership can the knowledge of the soul emerge and our fullest potential be attained.

The goal of all work, *of all service*, is simply to bring out what is already there, to unveil the soul.

CHAPTER ONE

The Nature of Service

During a Midwestern storm of rain, hail, lightning, and thunder, my mother stopped at the grocery store and asked me to run in for a loaf of bread. As I prepared to get out of the car, I noticed little Janie running down the street. She wore her usual tattered clothes, and her bald head, the result of some condition unknown to me, was unprotected from the hail. Many of our schoolmates teased her, judging her as inferior because of her poverty and appearance. I jumped out of the car and gave her my raincoat. She put it over her head and continued running.

I remember thinking, "I am here to help others." I was ten years old.

THE URGE TO SERVE

The urge to serve is the basic urge of the soul. From deep within us arises an inner desire to make a difference in the world by contributing to the well-being of our planet. Innately, we want to share ourselves and our talents with others through work, relationships, creative expression, and the alleviation of suffering.

This urge becomes evident in childhood, expressing itself in many forms. From an early age, children desire to help clean, garden, prepare food, and care for and even protect siblings. Adults also serve in the family through parenting and providing material security.

As individuals develop, they take the urge to serve beyond the family to church, school, community, and finally to the workplace. Their behavior in these places may not seem like service to them. They may simply respond to a desire to make someone feel better or to give something back out of gratitude and abundance. Making the community a better place to live and being a good student in order to become a capable adult both express the urge to serve. Some people may recognize that caring for their physical and emotional health is a service.

Service begins as an inner process rather than an outer action. The inner desire to care for oneself and to help others is deeply rooted in the unconscious and underlies the creation of all of life's "masterpieces." Not until we reach psychological and spiritual maturity, however, do we discover the profound depth of the dynamic inner process of our urge to serve.

This inner process is dependent upon the movement of our Life Force, an ever-present creative energy. This energy moves through us rather than being generated by us. Flowing naturally, allowing rather than imposing, the movement of this energy re-

Service begins as an inner process rather than an outer action.

sults in a series of transformations that move us from unconscious to conscious awareness. Our awareness of the Life Force deepens and expands, paralleling the unveiling of the soul.

As our awareness awakens even minimally, we recognize that this energy, by its nature, wants to move. A realization begins to dawn that by applying self-effort we can work with the Life Force to remove the obstacles within ourselves that inhibit the natural expression of our souls. When we apply our own effort, grace moves too, and the soul begins its journey of evolution. The greater our attention to this inner force, the more grace guides our lives.

When we apply our own effort, grace moves too, and the soul begins its journey of evolution.

The attraction of the outer world, however, is very strong and demanding. Through our many life experiences, we learn that when we close around the Life Force, keeping it within ourselves, it implodes. Implosion causes self-absorption, inertia, and lifelessness. If we do not allow this energy to move outward, we eventually use ourselves up, dying emotionally, mentally, and even physically.

To continue our evolution, we must share the newly awakened soul knowledge in some practical way. As we receive wisdom, we give it away unconditionally. As we give, we learn once again, purifying and refining the channel for the Life Force. During this ongoing process of giving and receiving, we open ourselves to the increased flow of this energy. We sense the Life Force growing larger, deeper, and stronger. The Life Force, of course, does not change. Rather, it transmutes us as we allow it to work through us. When we willingly allow the Life Force to move freely, offering no resistance or direction, it removes all obstacles to our healing and integration.

Each life experience confronts us with an opportunity to learn to cooperate with and use the Life Force. Prompted by the life event, the Life Force offers a **series of phases** through which to experience the dynamics of the interconnected relationships with ourselves, God, and others. These others may be people, groups, ideas, places, or objects.

Feelings of victimization, rage, resentment, and bitterness triggered by an event notify us of the opportunity to enter the first phase—the recognition of the need for emotional healing. With this recognition, we enter the phase of taking responsibility for our emotions, attitudes, and reactions. Responsibility entails understanding that no one and nothing outside us creates our perceptions and reactions.

Following this recognition, we enter a phase of acceptance of all of our attitudes and attributes, positive and negative. Acceptance cancels out any need to deny what has occurred or the roles that we or others play in the event. Acceptance allows entrance to the next phase—forgiveness of self and others, whether the harm done was intentional or unintentional. With forgiveness, we open the door to compassion for ourselves and those involved and can then extend compassion to all of humanity. By cooperating with the Life Force, we chisel away our misunderstanding and suffering and reveal the soul's knowledge.

In the final phase, a veil lifts as the Life Force energy helps us reach a resolution that transforms the painful experience into a gift. By way of these phases, the Life Force leads us to the recognition that compassion for our own humanness and suffering expresses as universal love for others. This recognition transmutes our very beings. The movement of the Life Force within us explains our innate desire to share the gifts of our own healing. The Life Force produces a constant and passionate drive toward full expression of each being's potential. This driving energy is why service is life itself and why we have an urge to serve.

The movement of the Life Force within us explains our innate desire to share the gifts of our own healing.

THE LAWS OF SERVICE

Synchronicity illustrates that minds are joined, that we are not separated and isolated from one another in the world.

Over time, from observing my life, I noticed there seemed to be a dynamic system of natural laws for bringing the soul's urge to serve into full expression. Once I identified these laws, I saw how they can sustain us through the ebb and flow of our individual and collective lives. Abiding by these laws allows us to honor rather than harm our planet, ourselves, and others. Practicing them supports our psychological and spiritual development and brings learning, clarity, and greater ease to our life of service.

The laws of service are visible in this event in my life:

> Early one Sunday morning I was driving to yet another personal growth workshop, which I hoped held the key for healing my wrenching emotional pain. On this particular morning, alienation and darkness engulfed me and I considered suicide my only recourse. As I drove through the Fillmore District of San Francisco, I noticed that the streets, like me, were empty of life.
>
> I stopped at a red light. Out of the corner of my eye I saw a woman dressed in her Sunday best crossing the street in front of me. To my surprise, she suddenly stopped and stood at the hood of my car. She then turned and smiled, her face beaming with love. Her look warmed my heart. The purity of her love kindled a memory of a love within me, a love forgotten and unreachable until that moment. I smiled. She turned and walked on.

This meeting took only seconds, yet it served as a catalyst for shifting my emotional state. Our interchange reminded me of the love of God within all humanity. With this awareness, I began the ascent out of my inner darkness.

Through the **law of synchronicity**, a seeming coincidence of time brought the woman and me together on a street corner. At an unconscious level, the person offering help, the woman, was attracted to me, the person calling for help. Naturally and without effort, we were drawn together to serve and be served.

Analyst Carl Jung wrote that at the level of the collective unconscious we are all connected in a meaningful way. This connection includes both animate and inanimate objects. Synchronicity illustrates that minds are joined, that we are not separated and isolated from one another in the world. The more we align with this connectedness, the more often synchronistic events appear in our lives. The law of synchronicity makes it possible for individuals to serve and be served with the "right amount" in the "right way" in the "right time" and "right place." This law works even when the person being served does not recognize or accept the gift and when the person offering service is not conscious of doing so.

The more we align with this connectedness, the more often synchronistic events appear in our lives. The law of synchronicity makes it possible for individuals to serve and be served with the "right amount"

The **law of *dharma*** establishes how we serve and whom we serve. *Dharma* is a term used in Eastern spiritual traditions and refers to two levels of duty. First, there is Eternal *Dharma*, a moral law of spiritual Truth applying to everyone and infusing every phenomenon. In Western thought, one's obligation to love God with all one's heart, soul, and mind is akin to Eternal *Dharma*. We serve God or are *Dharmic* when we practice Eternal Truth in our daily lives.

On the individual level, *dharma* is the practice of peace and service by doing our duty in the world from a place of right atti-

We are dharmic
when we
follow our
unique duty
and function.

tude. In Western thought, this is akin to loving our neighbor by doing our duty in the world. We are *dharmic* when we follow our unique duty and function. This law articulates God's purpose, mission, and vision for us as individuals and as groups of individuals. In this way, a person has *dharma* and groups or organizations have *dharma*.

The *dharma* of the woman in my story might have been that of a loving parent or grandparent. Her practice of Eternal *Dharma* became visible in the Divine Love she emanated to me.

The **law of omnipresence** ensures that service pervades all of life; everything is service. At all times we are serving and being served. Who serves us is not necessarily whom we serve, and how we serve is not necessarily how we are served. Time is also a factor. For example, we might be served today through a particular legacy of a relative who lived four or five generations ago. My interchange with the woman crossing the street was one in which I was served in a particular way. I may serve others in a different manner.

The **law of evolution** defines the levels of awareness of service within the seven stages of the evolution of the soul. Through the law of evolution we work toward integrating all aspects of ourselves as physical, emotional, mental, and spiritual beings. As we become fully integrated persons accepting of all aspects of ourselves, the light of the soul spontaneously pours into our consciousness. Our lower desires give way to higher ones. Our inner state becomes one of unconditionality and selflessness in action.

The quality of our inner state determines the quality of our service. The intent of our service determines the stage of soul development. The woman on the street beamed unconditional love and appeared devoted to God. Her selfless action conveyed

The quality of our inner state determines the quality of our service.

an inner state of one in an advanced evolutionary stage of service.

The quality of service is independent of the form of the service. Different persons can perform the same action with differing motivations. For example, one might serve the poor in order to assuage her guilt for not being poor herself while another might serve the poor as devotion to God.

Our awareness stage when being served corresponds to our awareness stage when serving. For example, those who serve while seeing the world from a right/wrong perspective will tend to judge the service they receive from others as being justified or unjustified. Those who serve while being self-responsible for their emotional reactions will be self-responsible for their emotional reactions when being served, viewing both the giving and receiving of service as opportunities for learning and growth.

At the time the woman on the street emanated Divine Love to me, I was feeling depressed, unloved, and unlovable. I was an empty vessel, which her love filled. The fact that someone I did not know could give me such love gave me hope for other relationships in my life. Because the love the woman radiated was unconditional, a second thing occurred. In that moment she showed me what it would feel like to be healed of my need to seek fulfillment outside myself. She gave me hope and she inspired my faith. I suddenly knew that what seemed impossible was actually possible.

The law of evolution also occurs on a group level. Groups engaging in the activity of service have a group consciousness formed by the collective inner states of the members. The group members' collective motivation for service determines the evolutionary level of the group's service.

The **law of receiving** ensures that we simultaneously receive what we have given. As a vessel, we are full when we allow the

Those who serve while being self-responsible for their emotional reactions will be self-responsible for their emotional reactions when being served, viewing both the giving and receiving of service as opportunities for learning and growth.

*Just as others
benefit from
the energy
of well-being
that emanates
from us as we
heal and grow,
they are
impacted by our
negative thoughts
and feelings.*

Life Force to continuously flow through us. To keep and strengthen what we have, the law of receiving demands that we must give it away. To give unconditionally, without expectation of reward, we must first unconditionally receive, accept, and integrate all that is given to us. Our ability to receive eventually dies when we are not open to receiving. The inability to fully receive arises from the ego's need to defend itself against love. In this painful paradox, we become narcissistic, focusing unceasingly on our lack and on our desperate need to have our vessel filled from the vessels of others.

In my story, I was willing to receive the gift of the woman's service. She was strengthened by the love she gave and by the love and gratitude that I reflected back to her.

The **law of uniformity** conveys that our service to another person is simultaneously offered as a gift to the whole of humanity. This occurs because we share a collective unconscious. I have often shared the story of the woman's love with others, some of whom were changed by it. Even if I had told no one, her gift of love affected both my consciousness and hers. This love became a pebble dropped in a pond, its ripples shifting the consciousness of people neither of us knew.

This law applies to our expression of negative states as well. Just as others benefit from the energy of well-being that emanates from us as we heal and grow, they are impacted by our negative thoughts and feelings. At the time of this incident, I saw that my angry and depressed mental state had moved out into the world and was impacting the well-being of others.

The **law of extension** ensures that we naturally become healers of that which we ourselves have been healed. What we extend is specific to our own healing. For example, a person healed of depression extends the possibility of healing for others who are depressed. I experienced an emotional healing when the woman in my story expressed love. For her to extend this healing, she had to have experienced it herself at some time in her life. In turn, I have extended my healing to others in the same way.

The **law of agreement** suggests the possibility that prior to incarnation souls can choose to make commitments to serve by playing a particular role in another soul's life experience. The agreements may be between individual souls, between an individual and a group, or among groups of souls.

In India there is a story of a disciple who begged his Master to bring the only son of his best friend back to life. The Master said he could do that, but first he wanted to explain the purpose of the boy's life. Prior to the parents' incarnations, a soul who loved them very much agreed that if they became lost in materialism, he would be born to them and rekindle the Divine Love they had forsaken. To provide the impetus for the needed change and growth, he agreed to die as a young child. The parents had become ruthless in their pursuit of materialism, living lives of wealth, fame, and success at the expense of others. Only the death of their beloved child would turn them inward.

Very possibly, my meeting with the woman had been prearranged. She might have agreed to meet me at a time when my life was in peril in order to remind me of the love I had forgotten.

The **law of transmutation** allows us to see the gifts of our experiences and operates in two major ways. First, it permits the energy of an initially negative experience or troubled state of mind to alchemically convert to the positive energy of learning and growth. Therefore, the initial negative energy of an experience is not necessarily synonymous with how that experience serves us. Events initially perceived as damaging to our well-being can serve us at a high level. Events can serve as the catalysts that enable

In the intensity of silence that is the soul's domain, we experience the depth of our strength.

our experiences to move over time to ever deeper levels of under-standing. Whether positive or negative, our experiences are dy-namic and embody layers of trust and wisdom. Outer events serve to stimulate the unfolding of new layers of understanding to our awareness.

In every moment we have the power to choose our attitudes, beliefs, motivations, and acts of service.

In my story, the woman's love was the catalyst that shifted me out of my depressed emotional state. My inner experience of dark-ness was transmuted to one of love and kindness. Through the law of transmutation, my troubled state of mind was converted to positive energy.

The **law of transcendence** assures us that we are served at a level of the soul that goes beyond human knowledge. The world of appearances, the material world, does not limit service. At a conscious level we recognize that we serve or are served in a spe-cific way by a certain event. At an innermost and unconscious level, however, the soul experiences that same event in a way that is separate from our conscious awareness. It is as though we have surpassed or transcended our sensory experience but not our spiri-tual knowledge. The soul awakens to a spiritual lesson or truth.

The soul's awakening to spiritual knowledge is a mystical ex-perience. In the intensity of silence that is the soul's domain, we experience the depth of our strength. The experience of the soul's awakening to its knowledge is thorough and comprehensive. Through spiritual intuition we bridge the unconscious and con-scious and reap the benefits of our inner experience. In some appropriate and needed way, we bring our newly discovered soul knowledge into the world.

Although I am unaware of the precise manner in which my soul was served by meeting the woman on the street, the event was a transcendental experience. Intuitively, I now know the power power of unconditional love that goes beyond the physical universe. I now remember to call upon this power in times of discouragement and self-negation. Spiritual intuition is an active presence in my life and in my service.

THE POWER OF CHOICE

The soul moves forward in its unfoldment through the power of personal choice. Choice, an activity of the will, is the vehicle we use to manifest our destiny in the world. In every moment we have the power to choose our attitudes, beliefs, motivations, and acts of service. By choice, we embrace the laws of service and respond to the urge to serve. By choice, we expand our understanding of the breadth and depth of service. By choice, we evolve psychologically and spiritually. In all ways, we choose service; service does not choose us.

Choice translates into change only when it is preceded by purpose and followed by action. Before making a choice, we look inward and contemplate our motivations and intentions. We ponder the aim or goal we want to reach. Once we choose our motive and affirm our intention, we develop and carry out a plan of action. This action is both outer and inner. Inner action of thought and contemplation precedes choosing the quality of our inner state. We may or may not decide to perform an outer action. In this context, however, inaction is a form of action.

We choose our action from among many possibilities. A choice reached without deliberation, examination, and evaluation of all aspects of the situation that confronts us can lead to impulsive and ill-advised action. When we make a choice, we simultaneously choose the consequences of that choice. The consequences or outcomes of our actions illustrate the power of our choices.

Service provides a context to choose to monitor our inner

Choice, an activity of the will, is the vehicle we use to manifest our destiny in the world.

*When we,
as servers,
focus on the
quality of
the mind,
service becomes
a powerful
classroom for
personal learning
and growth.*

state. We monitor our inner state by shifting the mind from an outer focus to an inner contemplation. This inner contemplation, in turn, allows us to investigate our motivations for serving. When we, as servers, focus on the quality of the mind, service becomes a powerful classroom for personal learning and growth. Such focus is an essential tool in using life experiences to awaken the soul and to establish congruence between inner motives and outer action.

To assist people in establishing this congruence between inner motives and outer actions, I identified ten principles called universal tributes. The word "tribute" refers to a gift given in gratitude, respect, and honor; giving a tribute requires intentionality. The "Universal Tributes" are therefore guidelines for serving with the highest possible intention. Each of the Tributes has tenets that provide steps for attaining the integration of inner state and outer action. The Tributes and their tenets are outlined completely in Part Two, Stage Five: Healing the Healer. It is not until that stage that one has the skills, commitment, and discipline to truly use the guidance of the Tributes.

Specifically, the Tributes reflect the unity of self and service and honor the partnership of the server and the one served. Through the Tributes, service reveals itself as a natural and effortless extension of the love of God, rather than a specific outward act. At its purest, service is unconditional; for our gifts to be freely received, they must be freely given. Service becomes a natural, integral, and ongoing part of every aspect of daily life. No longer is service viewed as a quality, a performance, something to strive towards, or something to use to salvage the world. The server and served are One, and this One includes sentient and insentient, visible and invisible, the personal God and the Unknowable Absolute.

The Universal Tributes

1. My life goal is to align my will with Divine Will and to increase the time I function in this state of Higher Knowing.

2. I know my chosen life's purpose is in alignment with a Higher Purpose for me when I am inspired and when I experience the joy, spontaneity, and gratitude of service.

3. Divine Will works through me as me when I have no attachment to the form of the task and no expectations of outcome.

4. By continually doing my inner work, I engender compassion for myself and others.

5. With honesty and kindness, I take responsibility for my own choices and allow others to do the same.

6. I use each encounter as a reflection of either a remembrance of Divine Love or a grievance I continue to hold against myself or another.

7. I acknowledge the reciprocal relationship between giving and receiving, understanding that both are essential for the well-being of myself and others.

8. I see the external reality of a situation as well as seeing beyond it to the personal lessons, inner strength, and spiritual essence of myself and others.

9. I support my healing process and that of others with patience, gentleness, and unconditional acceptance.

10. I accept the reality of the presence of Divine Love within my own mind and invite others to accept that same Love within themselves.

The word "tribute" refers to a gift given in gratitude, respect, and honor; giving a tribute requires intentionality. The "Universal Tributes" are therefore guidelines for serving with the highest possible intention.

When we truly serve, we draw upon the spiritual strength, the wisdom, and the directing power of our own soul and that of the person we are serving. The task to be done is always too big for our personality selves. The soul instinctively identifies with all that is good and naturally and effortlessly engages in the activity of service.

A partnership forms between the knowledge that resides within us and our outer life circumstances. By accepting the rigorous discipline of this partnership, our soul's essence emerges, and we attain our fullest potential.

SYNTHESIS

Life is service. The purpose of life, and thus of service, is to awaken the knowledge of the soul. The process of using our experience to awaken the soul crafts our destiny as surely as Michelangelo crafted a statue. A partnership forms between the knowledge that resides within us and our outer life circumstances. By accepting the rigorous discipline of this partnership, our soul's essence emerges, and we attain our fullest potential.

A meaningful and uplifting way to participate in the evolving world is to continually expand the breadth and depth of how we view ourselves and our relationship to service. The effect of this expanded focus on human interaction will be a higher vibration of service and a more compassionate and joyous way of life. We will begin to experience a greater connection with one another regardless of who we are or how we choose to live our lives.

Until we understand the cause of our suffering and have compassion for ourselves and others, the suffering on our planet will not cease. A new awareness of service can be the current that will carry us to shore. The purity of service is a direct expression of the purity of the motivation for serving. When collectively we understand service as an expression of a divine plan, we will no longer experience short-term solutions leading to new and greater problems. We will step off the cycle of suffering.

An ancient Chinese teaching reminds us that the state of the world is dependent upon the state of the nations, the state of the nations is dependent upon the state of the people, and the people begin with one. We are just beginning to understand the full meaning of Mohandas Gandhi's words, "He who would be a friend of God must either remain alone or make the whole world his friend."

The purity of service is a direct expression of the purity of the motivation for serving.

*C*HAPTER TWO

Service and the Evolution of the Soul

*I*n 1990 I went on a third pilgrimage to Medjugorje, a village in what was then Bosnia-Hercegovina, Yugoslavia. There, six visionaries have seen apparitions of the Virgin Mary since 1981. Whereas my first two visits were filled with awe and peace, a sense of dread pervaded this trip.

On the last day of my visit, a group of us stood outside the home of one of the visionaries. Someone pointed to upwards and said, "Look, it's the Madonna!" Across the sky I saw the Madonna watching two separate images.

In one image, a line of beings moved, ever-changing. At the head of the line was a baby boy; a young boy replaced him. Then in quick succession, each figure was replaced by an older one: adolescent, young man, middle-aged man, old man. A skeleton finally replaced the old man and the sequence began over again. In the adjacent image was a large hole. Through the hole, I could see a man, cupping his hands into a megaphone, speaking to us. I could not hear what he said.

I watched until night came and the vision vanished. Within weeks, the cruel and bitter civil strife known as the Bosnian War began its six year span.

THE PARAMETERS OF THE SOUL'S EVOLUTION

In the vision of Medjugorje, I witnessed the process of evolution of the soul. Science defines evolution as the progressive development of an increasingly complex system of structures. From a spiritual view, however, evolution involves more than "increasing complexity." "Evolution is best thought of as Spirit-in-action, God-in-the-making, where Spirit unfolds itself at every stage of development, thus realizing more of itself at every unfolding," says Ken Wilber, a leading writer on consciousness and transpersonal psychology. "Spirit is…the entire process of unfolding itself, an infinite process that is completely present at every finite stage." The process of unfoldment spirals from simplicity to complexity to simplicity once again. Just as Michelangelo's uncompleted statues are esteemed masterpieces of art, the soul at each stage of its release into being is perfect even though its full potential is not yet realized.

Early in our evolution, we lack awareness of the potential wealth of the soul's knowledge that resides within us. The inexperienced soul focuses on physical survival, acquires life experiences, and strives to master living in the world. Simplicity gives way to complex thought systems that attempt to create order out of chaos and to rationally explain the intricacies of all matters personal, social, and economic. The soul feels driven by an increasing need for competence and mastery of information, skills, and technologies.

From an evolutionary perspective, an individual always has an opportunity to move upward and outward on the spiral of life and inward and deeper on the quest for union with God. As the soul matures, it requires not greater complexity, but simplicity,

Just as Michelangelo's uncompleted statues are esteemed masterpieces of art, the soul at each stage of its release into being is perfect even though its full potential is not yet realized.

*When the
personality self
opens to the gifts
of the soul,
it receives
spiritual teachings
that embody
wisdom and
understanding.*

surrender, and *beingness* rather than *doingness*. Attention shifts away from the complexity of the material world and embraces the unknown. All things are accepted as simultaneously individual, interrelated, and a single united One. This acceptance allows action in the world without the barriers of categories, theologies, or philosophical constructs. Acceptance also allows the testing and challenging of the limits of one's own and others' beliefs. Established in a state of not-knowing, the soul breathes and its deeper knowledge emerges. When the personality self opens to the gifts of the soul, it receives spiritual teachings that embody wisdom and understanding.

As revealed in the teaching of my Medjugorje vision, multiple levels of reality are available to us at the same time we are evolving in the physical world. These alternative realities appear through dreams, synchronistic events, visions, intuitions, and even psychic phenomena. The willingness to embrace the unknown enhances our awareness and experience of these other realities. The Medjugorje vision suggests that important spiritual messages are always at hand and that, for whatever reason, we are not hearing.

At any time during one's life, an individual can choose to bring into consciousness aspects of the soul's knowledge. The soul's unfolding process is holographic in nature. A hologram is a three-dimensional image created by interacting light sources. When a hologram is divided, each part still contains the entire image within it, although each is from a slightly different perspective. A holographic construct of the soul and of human life means that every part reflects a vision of the whole. The soul's essence or wholeness is retained while simultaneously engaging in the process of unfoldment. The holographic reflection of the soul's unfoldment process and progress is visible in every individual and collective human action, decision, and relationship.

The soul is already complete and whole; what evolves is its awareness of its ever-present perfection. Physical death does not end the existence of the soul or its evolving awareness. As spiritual essence, it continues to grow after death of the physical body. The greater our conscious awareness of the many levels of our development and that our development extends beyond the material plane, the fewer detours we will make along the path of wholeness.

ASPECTS OF THE SOUL'S UNFOLDMENT

The soul is both nonmaterial and mysterious. It has one fundamental purpose and activity: to make knowledge manifest in the material world. Individually and collectively, the soul's desire to bring its knowledge into consciousness shapes the material world. Through the experience of time and space, the soul reveals its knowledge by engaging in a process of radiating unfoldment. The soul, like a stone dropped into a still pond, is a central point from which concentric waves emanate outward. The stillness of the pond represents clarity of intention. The greater the clarity, the farther the soul's knowledge radiates—to the body, to others, to the material universe, and beyond.

The soul's unfoldment process is cyclical in nature and its evolution entails numerous changes, steps, and characteristics. A common characteristic of the soul's unfoldment is its frequent return visits to lessons that on a conscious level we believe we have mastered. For example, we surprise ourselves by repeating a behavior long since abandoned. Although the pattern is the same, on the return visit we usually explore it with deeper awareness. Return visits of the soul are transcendent in that they help us to uncover a truth or nugget of wisdom not previously seen.

The soul's unfoldment process is cyclical in nature and its evolution entails numerous changes, steps, and characteristics.

*Even when the
personality self
is unconscious
and unaware,
the soul leads
it through
experiences that
focus on what
it is to learn,
contribute,
achieve, or
create in
this lifetime.*

Return visits are reminders that the soul's unfoldment is a process composed of steps and stages. The wisdom learned from each step is brought forward to the next. There are serious consequences from trying to skip over steps, particularly the psychological step of healing emotional wounds. When individuals fail to heal their inner conflicts and to glean wisdom from life lessons, they view the world through the veil of their unhealed and unintegrated self.

Another trait of the soul is that its process of evolution is unique to each person. By definition, individuals do not evolve with the same talents or tendencies nor at the same pace. Because appearances are unreliable sources of truth, we cannot assess the actual level of our own or another's soul even when appearances suggest a given stage of development. For this reason, comparison of spiritual attainment is impossible and is a product of either/or thinking leading to judgement of another's progress and service as better than or worse than our own.

The uniqueness of the soul is visible in the diverse purposes, missions, and destinies of different individuals. Even when the personality self is unconscious and unaware, the soul leads it through experiences that focus on what it is to learn, contribute, achieve, or create in this lifetime. Most of us spend the first part of life looking for fulfillment in our bodies, work, religion, and relationships. With maturity, we each experience an urge to follow our purpose, find our missions, and reveal our destinies. We look for ways to contribute, to put our imprint on the planet.

It is possible that prior to incarnation, our soul chooses the knowledge to learn this lifetime and makes agreements with other souls who are to help. The learning, or more accurately the unveiling of this knowledge, is our life **purpose**. Our life purpose is often visible as a theme running through our life experiences. For example, in doing a life review, one person noted how since childhood she has felt driven to find a way to communicate her inner being to others. As a child, she had a speech impairment, and at college she majored in English. Later, she studied communication disorders, and her first career centered on diagnosis of children with speech and language difficulties. Still later, the drive to express herself at deeper levels led her to express her essence by speaking and writing on psychological and spiritual growth.

One's **mission** is the context within which the soul's knowledge can be unveiled and is reflected in one's life circumstances, work, and relationships. Some people have very specific missions, such as being a carpenter, parent, teacher, or violinist. People who do not identify such a well-defined task often feel lost, disillusioned, and depressed. They may fear they will never discover their mission. The activities and circumstances that naturally draw one hold the answer to the quest.

If we develop the confidence to follow our intuition, we will fulfill our purpose, mission, and destiny.

A life mission, however, may not be what it appears to be. We may actually be doing our life's work while we are discovering what we think our life's work is. Our life's work is not always an external activity. If we demand that it be such an activity and it is not, we will be disappointed. For example, I may believe that my mission is to teach about service and I may feel very fulfilled by this activity. Yet, my actual life's work may involve a more subtle relationship, experience, or teaching that I engage in as I teach about service. If this is so, I could have chosen to fulfill my life mission in other ways. There is no right or wrong way to do our life's work. Even what seem like wrong turns can be necessary and useful exploration. Basically we are here to learn and we cannot help doing that.

Destiny is a life goal, the potential that one is to fulfill in this life. Some individuals, like Michelangelo, are aware of their destiny at an early age. For most of us, however, our destiny unfolds along with the soul's awareness. When we allow the Life Force to flow through us and ourselves to flow with it, we intuitively know what is right for us to do and what we do well. If we develop the confidence to follow our intuition, we will fulfill our purpose, mission, and destiny. If we ignore our intuition, then we go off course and may miss our opportunity. Even then, if we are willing to stay open to change, we can correct our course. Always, we can choose whether to follow our destiny.

Forward movement requires a conscious commitment to growth and with it the recognition that the hidden side of ourselves affects all aspects of our being and our soul's expression of service.

CYCLES OF LIFE

Evolutionary cycles exist within life and death. As revealed in the Medjugorje vision of the infant to skeleton sequence, developmental cycles pervade all levels of life—physical, mental, emotional, and spiritual. Over the course of life, one area of development may receive more focus or be a greater priority than another. After death, the evolutionary cycle continues in the form appropriate to the soul's journey.

A crucial integrative point in the cycle of the soul's unfoldment occurs when the physical, mental, emotional, and spiritual levels meet. At this point, the spiritual and human natures become one harmonious system. When this occurs, the soul's true desire becomes clear: to experience the presence of God in itself and in others.

STAGES OF AWARENESS OF THE SOUL

The soul moves through a series of cycles or stages on its journey to full expression. As we move through each stage of unfoldment, we experience two pulls of energy. We are perfect and complete where we are and so feel pulled to stay there. At the same time, the pull to keep moving is strong and so we feel pulled to ward the next stage. When we are conscious of these two inner pulls, we embrace the need to tend to our total well-being—physical, mental, emotional, and spiritual. To do this and to continue to evolve, we must acquire skills for dealing with the shadow, all that is unrecognized and unacknowledged within ourselves. Examining the shadow side of ourselves requires that the pull forward be stronger than the pull to stay where we are. Forward movement requires a conscious commitment to growth and with it the recognition that the hidden side of ourselves affects all aspects of our being and our soul's expression of service.

In this model, there are seven evolutionary stages of the soul, each of which reflects a shift in human consciousness regarding the concept of service. The stages are discussed in full in Part Two of this book.

In this model, there are seven evolutionary stages of the soul, each of which reflects a shift in human consciousness regarding the concept of service.

THE SEVEN STAGES OF THE SOUL'S EVOLUTION THROUGH SERVICE

STAGE	SOURCE OF VALIDATION
STAGE ONE: Awakening to Serve	Unfocused
STAGE TWO: Work Ethic	Work
STAGE THREE: Missionary Attitude	Social action, religion
STAGE FOUR: Wounded Healer	Relationships

Transition: From Outer to Inner Directed

STAGE FIVE: Healing the Healer	Moving toward True Self
STAGE SIX: Selfless Action	True Self

Transition: From Physical to Nonphysical

STAGE SEVEN: Beyond the Physical	The Absolute

As the soul matures, the focus of both attention and intention moves from being outer to being inner directed.

Stages One through Four are initiatory evolutionary steps that primarily involve looking outside oneself for validation and comfort. In Stage One, the individual tends to dabble in the many offerings of the outside world to see what might offer salvation; their search is unfocused and other-dependent. In Stage Two, the individual finds a focus in work, primarily because work answers immediate needs of food, clothing, and shelter as well as providing a consistent way to receive reliable outside validation. In Stage Three, as a means of self-identification, the individual focuses on social action, religion, or some other institutionalized form of correcting the wrongs of the world. In Stage Four, relationships provide a similar function. Individuals are highly motivated to be active and productive in the world in Stages Two through Four.

The outside world's inability to provide the inner salvation being sought leads to a crisis, usually in mid-life. If one successfully negotiates the crisis, *doingness* gives way to *beingness* and one enters the fifth stage.

Stage Five requires a commitment to attend to the quality of one's inner state while living and serving in the world. As this is achieved, one moves into Stage Six, where *beingness* and *doingness* become integrated. In Stage Six one *is* service and as such the soul selflessly manifests its knowledge in the world. Stage Seven acknowledges the continuing evolution of the soul through service after death.

Several factors are integral to the soul's evolution within each stage. These developmental components are physical, psychological, social, and spiritual in nature. One such component is the **state of the**

WILL COMPONENTS AND STAGE OF
PRIMARY DEVELOPMENT

Strong Will: Stages One, Two, Three
Skillful Will: Stages Two, Three, Four
Good Will: Stages One, Two, Three, Four
Transpersonal Will: Stages Five, Six

self that describes the state of the individual's inner life. The state of the self relates to the development of the aspects of the will—strong will, skillful will, good will, and Transpersonal Will. Another component is **world view**, the lens through which a person at each stage looks at the world. At each stage the **relationship with God** also shifts. The awareness of the soul grows as the individual addresses the issues of the shadow. At each stage, there are **predominant shadow issues** related to hidden motivations to address before the individual can progress. As the soul matures, the focus of both attention and intention moves from being outer being inner directed. Inner focus causes the **mode of service** to shift away from serving to meet personal needs to serving as an expression of the soul's knowledge.

DEVELOPMENTAL COMPONENTS
FOR EACH STAGE

State of the Self
World View
Relationship with God
Predominant Shadow Issues
Mode of Service

STYLES OF SERVICE

There are two major tendencies of human nature that determine the predominant style of service. These styles reflect a unique way of manifesting individual purpose, mission, and destiny in the world.

These styles can be seen as "waves" that, in most instances, overlap and support one another. First wave people are pioneers who "light the candle," initiating a movement or a shift of perspective affecting many. Second wave people prefer to "tend the candle" with steadfastness and patience, searching for depth rather than breadth in their service.

Although we have an inherent and predominant preference

First wave people are pioneers who "light the candle," initiating a movement or a shift of perspective affecting many. Second wave people prefer to "tend the candle" with steadfastness and patience, searching for depth rather than breadth in their service.

Although we have an inherent and predominant preference for one or the other style, at different times in our lives or in different circumstances we may elect to incorporate traits of our less preferred style.

for one or the other style, at different times in our lives or in different circumstances we may elect to incorporate traits of our less preferred style. For example, a friend of mine practices his first wave preference by being an entrepreneur. He established one restaurant, and once it was successful, left it to a manager and went on to establish another. He now owns many restaurants. He develops his second wave abilities, however, by teaching a class that he has continuously revised and deepened over the past eight years. In contrast, a woman with a second wave preference works as a human resources officer, contributing to the careful development of an exemplary program for her company. She exercised her first wave abilities by founding a local organization of human resources personnel to enable the sharing of expertise and programs.

Extroverted, inspired, and charismatic, those of the first wave emanate an aura of enthusiasm and commitment to a vision and mission that appeals to others. They usually do not attend to details and are not good administrators. They prefer to be instigators or visionaries of projects, but do not carry out or deepen the daily work. Those who have a first wave destiny may initiate a project and then leave it for second wave people to implement. At other times they start a project and remain connected to it as the carrier of the vision, continuing to generate the enthusiasm of others. People with first wave destinies tend to serve in crises and short-term situations. Their intention is to make their work available to larger and larger numbers of people. Their energy moves readily from one person or place to another. First wave individuals may or may not be highly spiritually evolved. They may, however, have a special spiritual assignment that they feel driven to fulfill.

Those with a second wave preference may or may not be visionaries. If they are, they willingly do the detailed and administrative tasks necessary. They follow through with commitment on a given project. They tend to stay in one place over a long period of time, refining and deepening their work. Usually they have little interest in attracting large numbers of people, but they want to serve the people they do attract well. They, too, may or may not be highly spiritually evolved. They may also have a special spiritual assignment they have agreed to fulfill. Educators, helping professionals, artisans, and administrators are often of the second wave.

A SHIFTING
CONSCIOUSNESS OF SERVICE

The turn of the century provides an opportunity to review the status of our evolution as individuals and as humankind. Our lives and the world at large seem increasingly complex, unpredictable, and dangerous. Technology appears to have caused the universe to speed up; under the demands of constant change, time itself seems to be in short supply. Increasing numbers of people feel a loss of control over outer circumstances. This feeling is compelling them to an intense search for well-being based on inner resources and for a shared reality that includes meaningful and appropriate service.

In the Western world we are in the process of learning that we are whole systems rather than a collection of independent parts. Instead of identifying ourselves as either "healers" or "people in need of healing," we are moving toward being equal partners, supporting one another in a search for physical, emotional, mental, and spiritual well-being. The fragility and beauty of human life and of the world's resources demand that we recognize our interconnectedness. As a global family, it is imperative that we

In the Western world we are in the process of learning that we are whole systems rather than a collection of independent parts.

accept our responsibility for one another and the planet.

We are preparing for the next shift of human consciousness: the realization that personal growth and service relate to the unfoldment of the soul. The relationship between personal growth, service, and the soul's evolution is dynamic and systemic and necessitates a shift in our awareness of service. The two facets of this shift are in symbiotic relationship: the development of individual consciousness in relation to service and the evolution of collective consciousness through service.

As we evolve, we learn that work and service are interrelated and interchangeable.

For this shift to occur, a new and dynamic holographic structure must emerge. Such a structure links people into a larger working whole while preserving the identities of participating members. This shift will occur as increasing numbers of people realize the interconnectedness of all aspects of life—economic, political, social, environmental, and so on—among all inhabitants of the earth. We evolve through service as service evolves through us.

I believe the collective soul requires ten specific shifts in individual awareness and behavior to move forward in its evolution through service. When a critical mass of individuals has made these shifts, the collective consciousness will evolve to the next evolutionary stage.

The first shift in awareness requires the recognition that the true source of equanimity is within, not outside us in other people, places, or things. The citizens of the developed countries of the Western world are discovering that the material world does not satisfy the inner need for peace of mind. The search for happiness outside ourselves in money, success, and relationships has preoccupied us. As the systems around us become increasingly complex, more people are choosing voluntary simplicity. With the realization that we can choose the extent to which we allow the material world to control us, comes increasing realization of the true source of our happiness.

As this awareness deepens, we realize that, used wisely, material well-being supports our urge to serve and enables us to leave the world a better place. Our desire to serve expresses naturally and reveals our humanness as surely as our desire for food, shelter, and clothing. As each individual soul evolves in equanimity and shares this inner peace in service, the collective consciousness rises. Collectively, service evolves to a new level at which we no longer view it as separate from our natures and outside ourselves.

The second shift involves the recognition that the highest good for one must include the highest good for all. This shift moves us away from preoccupation with getting our individual needs met at the expense of others. Developmentally, we learn to honor the spiritual assignments of the lives of others as well as of our own lives. To fulfill our assignments, we do whatever needs doing in the moment. We willingly give up attachments to the gratification, form, and outcome of our work. Collectively, service evolves into a global and universal concept in which the good of the whole is valued above the immediate needs of the parts.

The third shift is the recognition that work is synonymous with service and necessary to our experience of harmony and joy. This shift contrasts with viewing work as separate from service and alien to our social, emotional, and spiritual well-being. As we evolve, we learn that work and service are interrelated and interchangeable. As we develop, we play different roles. Relationship (child, spouse, parent, and so on) defines some roles, while work (laborer, teacher, student, scientist, monk, and so on) defines others. Both categories of roles require effort and both earn intrinsic and extrinsic rewards. Essentially then, both categories are ones of "work." Through these roles we continuously serve and are served individually and on com-

The relationship between personal growth, service, and the soul's evolution is dynamic and systemic and necessitates a shift in our awareness of service.

munity, national, international, environmental, and global levels. Our work provides the medium for our service.

As consciousness develops and expands on both individual
and collective levels, the ways in which work serves to provide
daily opportunities for personal insight, growth, and service also
expand. Increasingly, work and worker, served and server meld
until the need for differentiation disappears.

Resisting the process of evolution leads to inertia of life energies and failure to develop potential.

**The fourth shift involves moving from either/or to both/
and thinking**. A systemic approach to well-being views individuals as whole systems rather than as a collection of independent parts. The systemic model focuses on solutions, on inclusion, on wholism, and on the assumption that each person is
doing the best he or she can with the information at hand. This
contrasts with the linear cause and effect model that polarizes
everything into either/or, right/wrong, better/worse, and superior/
inferior categories.

Categorizing and labeling who deserves service results in compartmentalization and biases our experience of the inclusiveness
of service. The focus has been on who "needs" service, such as
the poor, the disabled, the sick, the aged. As we become inclusive, we move into True Service, which recognizes the universal-
ity of service and the oneness of server and served. True Service is
also holographic. In a holographic model, any thought or belief
resides in and affects every aspect of life, not only certain parts.
Individually and collectively, we experience holographic thinking through the practice of living service in all aspects of our lives.

**Shift five involves seeing beyond appearances to the deeper
spiritual meaning**. This shift replaces belief in the limitations of the
material world. As we progress developmentally, we perceive the
same life event differently as we uncover truer and clearer levels of
awareness and interpretation. Nothing changes but our perceptions.

In the same way, how we serve and how we are served are not always as they appear to be. One cannot tell the level of someone's soul development from the outer form of their service. The motivation behind the serving, however, reflects the level of the soul's striving. Our motivations and our inner states change as our souls unfold. Our purpose and mission emerge as a natural extension of our work.

Collectively, service evolves to a place of recognition of and support for each individual's life purpose and mission. Additionally, group support enhances the individual's potential for reaching the ultimate spiritual goal of devotional service. The effect is cumulative. Over time, we feel increasingly connected to the spiritual essence of all humanity and to God.

The sixth shift is the recognition that answers lie on the level of cause and not on the level of effect. Developmentally, we move from searching for answers in the effects of our actions through judgement and blame to taking responsibility for our projections and searching for the cause within ourselves. At the place of cause, we can truly correct faulty perceptions and make new choices. Resisting the process of evolution leads to inertia of life energies and failure to develop potential. As we progress, the surrender of the self to the unknown becomes inevitable.

Collectively, service evolves to a model of individual self-responsibility functioning through group action. Through self-responsibility, individuals and groups set clear boundaries and well-defined goals.

Shift seven involves responding from the Witness Self on the mental level. This shift contrasts with reacting to life events from the emotional level. In early stages of development, we deny our feelings or become lost in them. We frequently create emotional bonds with others by sharing the pain of our wounds. Per-

One cannot tell the level of someone's soul development from the outer form of their service. The motivation behind the serving, however, reflects the level of the soul's striving.

*By focusing on
the means of
our healing
rather than
the end goal,
we free ourselves
to use all
available energy
to live in the
present moment
and be service.*

sonal growth entails self-discipline and self-responsibility. Accomplishing this requires learning to use and strengthen the Witness Self, that part of our psyche that can observe ourselves without judgement. In this way we learn to acknowledge our feelings, detach, and move on. As we grow, we no longer bond from our wounds but from our strengths and inner beings.

Collectively, this shift moves us away from the emotional view of service as a morally "right thing" performed to raise a group's status and sense of well-being. Instead, service is viewed inclusively: everything is spiritual, service is life, and God is One-in-All. At higher soul levels, God is simply One.

Shift eight is the awareness that True Service means being in the world at all levels of participation. This shift contrasts with the belief that True Service is only possible if one withdraws from the world. At early evolutionary stages, all-or-none thinking polarizes how we view and experience the world. We believe that being spiritual demands that we renounce the world and avoid participating in its pleasures. As our souls progress, we realize that spiritual development is without consequence unless we turn the energy of inward growth back out to flower in the external world.

Collectively, with this shift, service evolves into a generator of perpetual motion. As individuals and groups use their service to expand inwardly, the energy expands and moves out to effect change on all levels of life.

Shift nine states that acceptance of a higher calling of service means not so much being *of* service as *being* service. This shift challenges the view that inner work and spiritual connection are ends in themselves. Developmentally, we move away from viewing our personal healing as a way to "get better so we can get on with our lives." As our souls expand, we understand that wherever we are, however we are, and whatever we do *is* our life in that moment. We do not "get better" so much as we let go of the judgements we hold against ourselves. This inner work itself is our service; we serve as we work on our own healing. By focusing on the means of our healing rather than the end goal, we free ourselves to use all available energy to live in the present moment and *be* service.

Collectively, our individual explorations and adventures, engaged in consciously and with a higher purpose as our goal, serve the collective good. In the Greek myth, Hercules performed the Twelve Labors necessary to gather the Golden Apples of Hesperides with the intent of achieving immortality. As he overcame the challenges, he conquered his emotions and faced failure. As a consequence, he was able to use humility, overcome glamour, see through the veils of illusion, and have compassion. The fruit of his adventures was the bringing of these virtues into consciousness for others to acquire and use.

Shift ten involves aligning the personal will with the Transpersonal Will and allowing our destiny to unfold. The importance of this shift is evident when contrasted with using the personal will as an attempt to manipulate, control, or create our destiny. The evolution of the soul mirrors development of the aspects of the will: strong will, skillful will, good will, and finally alignment with the Transpersonal Will, the place where our will meets Divine Will. As we mature, we strengthen each aspect of will until we can bring them into balance. Once the aspects become balanced, we can call on whatever aspect we need in a given situation. Collective will motivates powerful change in groups, impacting everything from neighborhood associations to international politics. Each organization, city, and nation has a destiny; the collective will paves the path to that destiny or away from it.

As we mature, we strengthen each aspect of will until we can bring them into balance. Once the aspects become balanced, we can call on whatever aspect we need in a given situation.

SYNTHESIS

Care of the soul of humanity begins with the care of the individual soul.

As individuals learn and grow, they manifest their soul's knowledge in the world with a greater sense of purpose, mission, and destiny. As the number of advanced souls increases, a natural shift occurs in the collective consciousness of service. From pre-occupation with their own needs, people become concerned for themselves *and* for humanity as a whole. As acknowledged members of a global family, their lives are ones in which they recognize that true strength is inner strength and that the highest good for one includes the highest good for all.

Care of the soul of humanity begins with the care of the individual soul. As we develop and mature emotionally and spiritually, our service deepens and broadens. We call forth from within ourselves the resources needed in the moment. We learn to do this gradually as we move through the evolutionary stages of our awareness of service.

CHAPTER THREE

The Dimensions of Service

In the seventy-three seconds prior to the explosion that killed the seven astronauts aboard the space shuttle Challenger in 1986, one was recorded saying to another, "Let me hold your hand."

SERVICE AND SPIRITUAL TRADITIONS

In Michelangelo's painting of the Creation of Adam in the Sistine Chapel, he personified God as a Wise Old Man enveloped in a womb filled with angels. With one arm around the unborn Eve, who symbolizes the soul, He gazes at His own hand as He points a directive finger of Divine Power toward the hand of Adam. Adam, naked and alone, seems to search the face of God. He lounges with his arm propped on his knee and barely lifts his own index finger toward God's. Their fingers do not touch; there is a void between the hand of God and the hand of man. If Adam were only to lift his finger a fraction of an inch, he could touch God. Eve awaits joining Adam, looking toward him with anticipation. Through her, the Soul of God will birth into material reality.

One's inner call to God is the call to live a life of love through service.

Michelangelo's painting depicts God-waiting—waiting for us to "lift a finger" to touch the Absolute. When we lift a finger on our own behalf or on behalf of another, we are in service. We reach out to touch another's hand and our souls connect. In that moment, we touch God.

From diverse religious teachings we can distill two essentials: that union with the Absolute is possible and that service is a means to that union as well as its ultimate and highest expression. One's inner call to God is the call to live a life of love through service. Responding to this call initiates one's spiritual quest and is the work of a lifetime. Pastoral psychologist Bernard Groeschel writes, "When the individual has decided to respond to the call of God experienced within, and strives to make this call the center of activity and choice, he or she may be called a truly spiritual person."

We look at service through different lenses depending on religious training, culture, societal values, and the form of the service itself. The world's five major religions—Buddhism, Christianity, Hinduism, Islam, and Judaism—identify four primary dimensions of service: duty, charity, purification, and devotion.

To serve more consciously and to move ever closer to spiritual union, one must explore, develop, and integrate the qualities of these dimensions within oneself. The potential of each dimension is present in each stage of the evolution of the soul; however, each dimension receives more or less attention depending on our stage of development. Therefore, if we do not acquire a basic understanding of service as duty, we cannot practice service as charity, purification, or devotion. The first four stages (Awakening to Serve, Work Ethic, Missionary Attitude, and Wounded Healer) focus on exploring, understanding, and integrating service as duty and as charity. It is in Stage Five, Healing the Healer, that one begins to comprehend service as purification or as devotion. While we integrate these attributes progressively in the order presented here, we also are always deepening our understanding of all four.

In every religious tradition, one serves others at more and more sublime levels as one loves and serves God. These dimensions make up the curriculum of spiritual learning. No matter what the outer form of our spiritual path, we move from unenlightened to enlightened, from being caught in the world's illusion to being spiritually liberated, and from chaotic, antisocial behavior to mystic union and True Service.

No matter what the outer form of our spiritual path, we move from unenlightened to enlightened, from being caught in the world's illusion to being spiritually liberated, and from chaotic, antisocial behavior to mystic union and True Service.

SERVICE AS DUTY

The dictionary defines duty as an obligation, responsibility, assignment, or task. Through duty we willingly set aside our personal and individual interests for a wider good; through duty we show honor and respect to some authority beyond ourselves. Duty demands discipline, a self-controlled pattern of behavior.

We commonly associate duty with rigidity, constraints on individual freedom, and even punishment. Around the world there are religious and politically based sects that make adherence to duty and rules the principal responsibility of members. Many who experience the negative attitudes and punitive approaches of these groups resist the concepts of duty and of service as duty. Yet it is duty that is the basis for heroic acts, that pushes us to take risks, and that often brings out the best that is human. Through duty we just do what needs to be done. In its highest form, duty is the moment when our will meets God's Will, and we act in total consciousness but without analysis, judgement, or expectation of reward.

Discipline is an integral part of duty. It arises from knowing what we desire to achieve and from our willingness to perform what it takes to get there. If we want a healthy body, we practice discipline of diet and exercise. If we want a happy child, we discipline ourselves to develop the attributes of a good parent. If we want union with God, we follow a spiritual discipline. Through applying discipline, we perform our duties and obligations whether or not we desire to do them. We pay taxes, we sit through endless Little League games and PTA meetings, we tithe to the church or temple even when the electric bill is overdue. We give up personal pleasure and individual freedom for a higher end. The extent to which we do our duty willingly is the extent to which it is service and not sacrifice.

Service as duty begins at home. Here, religious and cultural teachings direct the behavior of adults and the teaching of children. The role and value of service as duty thus passes from generation to generation. This ensures the care of the unfortunate, respect for elders, the upholding of a communal good, and the

In its highest form, duty is the moment when our will meets God's Will, and we act in total consciousness but without analysis, judgement, or expectation of reward.

*The **strong will** is that aspect of the will needed for concentration, one-pointedness, and courage. Without the energy of the strong will, we would be unable to carry out our decisions and bring about our goals. Strong will manifests through self-discipline and individual responsibility.*

maintenance of religious practices and traditions. By attending to duty, we develop the strong will. The **strong will** is that aspect of the will needed for concentration, one-pointedness, and courage. Without the energy of the strong will, we would be unable to carry out our decisions and bring about our goals. Strong will manifests through self-discipline and individual responsibility. The practice of duty by giving, good works, spiritual practice, and as a container for all of life also develops other aspects of the will. Through development of the will, we arrive at the highest expression of duty, complete surrender to God.

DUTY AND GIVING

Service, at its simplest, is the relationship of giving and receiving. Although many of us were taught that it is more blessed to give than to receive, the two are indivisible. We cannot give if another does not receive nor can we receive if no one gives. Giving is a spiritual discipline; the gifts of learning to give freely and joyfully are transformative. The more we give unconditionally, the more is given to us to receive. This is true whether one gives money, time, or love. Through giving we learn and practice **good will**, that aspect of the will that enables us to abide by values and ethics that support good for ourselves and others.

Giving as duty begins for most with the fulfilling of religious and social obligations to the less fortunate. However unconsciously, most of us realize that our own well-being is dependent on the well-being of those around us. We give to the United Way or the Red Cross or we tithe to a religious organization. In Judaism, "righteous giving" is a gift of money, a tithe important in itself. Righteous giving is a way to be self-respectful; even the very poor need to tithe to someone less fortunate than themselves.

Tithing follows an ancient Judaic dictum to give one-tenth of one's income for the support of the priesthood, costs of the Lord's feasts and rituals, and the care of the poor. Those of other faiths also practice tithing. When one tithes, one gives a minimum of one-tenth away before one does anything else. One does not ask, "Do I have enough to give?" Practicing tithing as a duty brings the disciple face-to-face with any fear of lack and any obstacle placed in the way of experiencing the abundance of God.

Moses Maimonides, a preeminent Jewish intellectual of the twelfth century, wrote about the need to perfect oneself in the service of God. He desired to maintain the dignity of the poor and to follow the biblical dictum to tithe. He delineated eight levels of giving in order of worthiness.

*Through giving we learn and practice **good will**, that aspect of the will that enables us to abide by values and ethics that support good for ourselves and others.*

- Not giving; this is unacceptable.

- Giving grudgingly, reluctantly, or with regret.

- Giving cheerfully, but less than is appropriate.

- Giving appropriately when asked.

- Giving significantly before being asked.

- Giving without knowing to whom one gives, but the recipient knows the identity of the donor.

- Giving when one's identity is not known.

- Giving when neither giver nor receiver knows one another's identity; this is the highest and greatest level of giving.

DUTY AND GOOD WORKS

Duty also plays a significant role in the performance of good deeds, such as providing food, shelter, and other support for the sick and destitute. Jews, the Society of Friends, and the Unitarian Universalists, among many others, practice what the Jews call "repair of the world." These are good works dedicated to bringing peace, freedom, and social justice to all people. Some groups expand the concept to include humane treatment of animals or environmental causes. Performing such works broadens our perspectives and takes us out of self-centered daily concerns. Through good works we are able to walk a mile in someone else's moccasins, coming face-to-face with suffering.

In Buddhism, it is one's duty to acquire a right understanding of the cause of suffering, to be nonattached to suffering, and to practice altruism based on love and compassion. No matter what one's spiritual path, exploration of suffering is necessary because True Service can only arise when one is not attached to one's own or another's suffering.

By performing our duty to help our fellow humans, saving the environment, or otherwise promoting peace and compassion, we are acknowledging our connection with all beings, sentient and insentient. No matter what our religious orientation, all of creation is a manifestation of the one creative force. As receivers of this gift, we have a duty to honor and care for the interconnected system of which we are a part.

DUTY AS A CONTAINER FOR LIFE

In addition to tithing and good works, we can use duty consciously to provide a container for life itself. Some religious cultures, like the Islamic, Hasidic, and Amish, do not separate the sacred from the secular. Duty defines all of life through precepts and prohibitions interwoven into all aspects of family, civil, business, and personal life. Religious teachings prescribe strong communal ties and service to others. Members spontaneously gener-

No matter what one's spiritual path, exploration of suffering is necessary because True Service can only arise when one is not attached to one's own or another's suffering.

ate expressions of these teachings out of duty and faith and out of strong belief in their efficacy. The monastic orders of each religion also use duty in this way. The monastic life forces one to learn control and mastery of feelings, emotions, and desires. This involves the development of the **skillful will**.

The skillful will is that aspect of the will by which one identifies and directs one's inner thoughts, beliefs, and interests. The skillful will acts to elevate the lower motives. By engaging the skillful will, one learns how to use the least amount of energy to attain the desired result.

Fortunately, one does not need to live in a monastery to develop the skillful will or to use duty as a container for life. "Right living" or *dharma*, as explained under the Law of *Dharma* in Chapter One, is an inclusive concept of duty integral to Eastern philosophies. The concept is helpful in moving beyond the limitations of duty as adherence to rules and regulations.

Hinduism defines four stages of life: the stage of student, the stage of householder, the stage of forest dweller, and the stage of renunciate. No matter what role we play or how we choose to play it, it is our duty in that moment to fulfill its highest purpose and potential with integrity, responsibility, and intention. Our true duty is to recognize the God within us and to acknowledge that Truth for everyone else as well. Through attending to one's *dharma*, the mind becomes impartial to the outcome and is therefore free.

The concept of *dharma* teaches that we can dedicate everything we do to God. Every role we play, each interaction, each period of our lives has its time and purpose. When we see each moment as *dharma*, we stay focused without thinking we should be somewhere else doing something else. Duty as a container for life is a basic premise of True Service.

*The **skillful will** is that aspect of the will by which one identifies and directs one's inner thoughts, beliefs, and interests. The skillful will acts to elevate the lower motives. By engaging the skillful will, one learns how to use the least amount of energy to attain the desired result.*

DUTY AND SPIRITUAL PRACTICE

Because duty is an attribute of service and service reflects our relationship with God, duty has its place in our devotional life. Prayer, meditation, chanting, incense offering, and other such practices are spiritual "disciplines" because their benefit derives from consistent and unquestioning practice.

Through the practice of a spiritual discipline, we progressively surrender ourselves to God by means of constant self-examination and assessment of priorities. We engage in a spiritual discipline for its own sake, not to achieve enlightenment or any particular spiritual experience. Such a practice requires the integration of strong will, good will, and skillful will. As this integration occurs, we increasingly experience ourselves as aligned with the **Transpersonal Will**. The Transpersonal Will reflects the timeless, unchanging, eternal qualities of God. When aligned, we express our divinity in all that we think, do, and say. In this state we are willing channels through which powerful energies can flow and operate through our will-in-action.

The **Transpersonal Will** *reflects the timeless, unchanging, eternal qualities of God. When aligned, we express our divinity in all that we think, do, and say. In this state we are willing channels through which powerful energies can flow and operate through our*

SERVICE AS CHARITY

The word charity derives from the Latin *caritas*, meaning "love for our fellows." Synonymous with altruism, compassion, and unconditional love, charity is the kind of love that exhibits unselfish concern for, and total acceptance of, another. Some religions view charity as the human reflection of God's love for us. In others, it is the expression of awareness that we are not many, but One, and that whatever we do to one touches all.

Most of the world's religions express some form of the "golden rule," to treat others as we would like them to treat us; this is charity. Although expressed as philanthropy and good works, charity is more than that. For a Christian, it is the emulation of Jesus who served the sick, dying, oppressed, and outcast without judgement. For the Buddhist, it is the capacity to look at all living beings with eyes of compassion while acting in a way that relieves suffering. To truly serve with charity requires an understanding of the relationship between the state of being of the server and the quality of the service. This understanding unfolds as the soul evolves and is the soul's highest expression.

There are many obstacles on the way to complete expression of charity, many of which have to do with our motivations for serving. We may serve out of guilt, fear, pride, or to gain esteem from others or from God. Whatever the obstacles to charity, they are the obstacles to loving God. Charity requires that we give without attachment to the outcome of our giving, without expectation of reward, and without need of recognition. Achieving this level of surrender of personal desire requires constant vigilance of our inner being and of the quality of our service. To express true charity, we must purge deeply rooted and repressed inner conflicts.

Whereas tithing exemplifies doing one's duty by giving money or goods to support others, charity requires face-to-face giving and personal involvement. The concept of charity is the foundation of volunteerism, which serves the sick, dying, homeless, and helpless on community, national, and international levels. It is only through facing the suffering of others directly that we can face our own feelings, emotions, prejudices, and attitudes about suffering.

The Vietnamese Buddhist Thich Nhat Hanh teaches that one cannot be free of suffering unless one is willing for all others to be free. In his concept of "engaged Buddhism," one strives to *be peace* in all actions, from smiling and drinking tea to feeding hungry children and rebuilding war-torn villages. An engaged Buddhist is

Some religions view charity as the human reflection of God's love for us. In others it is the expression of awareness that we are not many, but One, and that whatever we do to one touches all.

one who brings the Buddhist practices of meditation, mindfulness, and compassion into all aspects of personal, interpersonal, social, and political life. For the engaged Buddhist, the practice itself is charity and charity is the practice.

Acts of charitable giving have the power to purify the soul. This is true because giving and receiving are inseparable.

Charitable love is a state of *being* turned toward action rather than an emotion or feeling. Christianity equates the love of God with the love of self and others. Christian teachings ask disciples to give of the least that they have, offering more than is requested. If attacked, they must turn the other cheek and use love as the only weapon against evil. Hinduism teaches that *seva* or selfless service is an expression of devotion to God. One serves selflessly because the love of God and others exceeds the love of self. Buddhism uses the term *dana*, the Sanskrit term for the perfecting of selfless, unconditional giving. Because *dana* reflects the spiritual truth that giving is a response to what is happening in the present moment, it is an expression of the devotion to Eternal *Dharma*. Judaism and Islam also place importance on giving without knowledge of to whom one gives and giving without expectations, hesitancies, and judgements.

Acts of charitable giving have the power to purify the soul. This is true because giving and receiving are inseparable. When we give freely and spontaneously, the supply of what we have to give for ourselves and for those we serve is unlimited. Likewise, when we receive openly, without reservation, we give back through gratitude, and we keep the cycle of giving and receiving flowing. This cycle is the creative force of life itself.

To take rather than receive and sacrifice rather than give blocks the cycle. Those who take rather than receive operate from the premise that there is a limit to universal abundance and that they must fight to claim what they feel they deserve. As a result, they grasp in the fear that nothing more will be available. Like fresh water poured into a swamp, the gifts given become tainted and can even cause illness. Those who insist on only giving and not receiving operate under the illusion that giving necessitates sacrifice. As a result, they feel they will lose something if they give it away.

True charity always helps the person who gives as much as it helps the recipient. To establish this reciprocal relationship, we must master four skills of giving: giving the right amount, giving the right thing, giving for the right reason, and giving at the right time. As mastery of the skills occurs, the giver opens to receiving. By modeling adept giving and receiving, the giver also makes it possible for those who receive his or her service to begin to master the skills of giving and receiving for themselves.

GIVING THE RIGHT AMOUNT

Whether we give money, time, or healing energy, we must be sensitive to what the recipient is able to receive. Given more than he feels he deserves, a person may respond with anger, guilt, or resentment. Given more than she can skillfully handle, a person may feel overwhelmed by the responsibility and waste the gift.

Intuiting the right amount to give requires connecting with the recipient. As the person opens to receiving the gift, he naturally accepts more of what is given. For example, in designing a lesson, a teacher matches the level and amount of the subject matter to the mental, emotional, and spiritual readiness of the student. She does not attempt to teach advanced algebra to first graders or expect medical interns to learn the intricacies of heart surgery from one lecture. Likewise, counselors and therapists learn not to attempt to lead clients to insights they are not yet prepared to hear. Giving the wrong amount creates resistance to receiving.

Those who insist on only giving and not receiving operate under the illusion that giving necessitates sacrifice.

When the heart desires to give money or time to a person or organization, the right amount will spring to the mind in the moment. The giving will not feel like a sacrifice, and it will cause no hardship. Only the giver can judge what this amount is. Fear of lack may create doubts about following the impulse of intuition. By following the practice of overriding such doubt, we experience the joy of giving and feelings of lack gradually disappear.

GIVING THE RIGHT THING

To give the right thing necessitates understanding that True Service expands peoples' choices rather than makes the choices for them.

We cannot know what is right for another person. My solution to your problem or your solution to mine may hinder more than help. To give the right thing necessitates understanding that True Service expands peoples' choices rather than makes the choices for them.

Unfortunately, religious and governmental efforts to serve often counterbalance an expanded choice with a decreased choice. In Alaska, the United States government offered education to the natives (more choice) but required that the formerly nomadic villagers remain in the village year round (less choice). Likewise, in Africa, missionaries offered health care (more choice) but required religious conversion (less choice). Although such choices reduced the incidence of disease, increased literacy, and provided connection with the larger world, they contributed significantly to the breakdown of indigenous societies and to feelings of helplessness among the people.

Understanding that the right thing is an offering of choices prevents the giver from becoming attached to the outcome of the service. For example, if the managers of a homeless shelter are attached to the outcome of their service, they become upset by those homeless who choose not to use the shelter. The managers may feel they have failed or that they are responsible for persuading the homeless to stay. On the other hand, if the managers understand that they are offering a choice rather than a shelter, then the responsibility for choosing remains with the individual homeless person.

Choice is also important for those who give. Servers need to explore what the "right thing" is to give. By exercising conscious choice of the gift, we give from abundance and meet our own needs as well as the needs of those we serve.

GIVING FOR THE RIGHT REASON

The right reason for giving is unconditional love unfettered by expectations of reward or response. Giving for the right reason requires a blending of duty and charity. Sometimes the reason to give is simply that a job needs doing. Such cases present opportunities, sometimes difficult ones, to learn to give without harboring any resentments or expectation of reward. Such challenges include risking one's life to save another's or accepting responsibility for the long-term care of aging parents.

The other reason to give is one that serves the server by being a natural expression of talents and interests. It is from the treasury of our own gifts that we find fulfillment and joy in giving.

GIVING AT THE RIGHT TIME

Timeliness is critical to maximizing the effectiveness and impact of service. Even when the amount, the rightness, and the reason for the gift are all correct, the gift may be given too soon or too late for the highest good of the receiver. Learning right timing involves developing trust in one's intuition and in the guidance of the True Self. Fortunately, the gift is never lost but is suspended in space and time; when the receiver is ready, she or he may elect to remember and accept the gift.

It is from the treasury of our own gifts that we find fulfillment and joy in giving.

*By using service
as a mirror,
it is possible to
identify and
then remove
the obstacles
we place
in the way of
recognizing our
true identity.*

Many years ago a colleague introduced me to an Eastern spiritual organization of which she was a board member. Through her influence, I met many of the group's leaders and received multiple, privileged opportunities. Instead of feeling grateful, I became confused, overwhelmed, and resistant. I questioned her motives and the motives of the group's leaders, feeling they welcomed me because of her influence, not because of my own merit or person. I questioned whether I participated out of her choice or out of mine. I doubted what I was given (the right thing), how much I was given (the right amount), why I was given privileges (the right reason), and why I was given them now in my life (the right timing). Only years later did I see how powerfully my colleague had served me. In my own timing and in my own way I came to accept the gifts of this organization as spiritually right for me.

SERVICE AS PURIFICATION

Through the conscious practice of service as duty and as charity, we increasingly let go of personal desires and stay focused on the desire of the soul. Service then becomes not only the extension or result of our spiritual development but the means for the soul's purification and evolution. By using service as a mirror, it is possible to identify and then remove the obstacles we place in the way of recognizing our true identity.

Service as purification is the place where outer action and inner truth become one. Purification is the direct result of spiritual discipline. Initially, we carry the spiritual discipline of prayer, meditation, and contemplation into daily activity. One example is the practice of prayer without ceasing. Soon, however, the discipline includes the use of the action itself as a source of insight. For example, each of the four kinds of yoga provides a different way to remove the layers of ignorance covering the knowledge of our true identity. *Karma* yoga uses work, *jnana* yoga the intellect, *bhakti* yoga the emotions, and *raja* yoga uses introspection. Service as purification requires constant attention to our inner state, emotions, thoughts, reactions, and physical sensations. Simply by paying attention, insights arise and inner shifts occur that affect outer action.

The practice of what Japanese Zen Buddhists call *takuhatsu* exemplifies service as purification. In this *dharmic* practice, monks, with bowls in hand, beg for alms. Having no expectations, they unconditionally receive what they are given, usually rice and money. Their willingness to do this practice with anonymity, without desire to look at the giver or to give something in return, tests the purity of their intentions. Those who practice *takuhatsu* also offer those who give alms an opportunity to test the purity of their intentions. The one who gives has an opportunity to practice doing so with no hesitancy, no desire for recognition, and no thoughts of concern, speculation, or judgement. Because it benefits giver and receiver, this form of giving is *Dharmic*. It is a practice of Eternal Truth.

Purification occurs in different ways and on many levels, depending on the developmental stage of the individual. Although service as purification does not occur until Stage Five, purification acts on other levels throughout our development. Different religions describe the evolution of the soul in different ways, yet in each, moving from stage to stage depends on purification. As the individual is purified so is the quality of his or her service; as the service is purified, so is the individual.

The construct provided by Bernard Groeschel identifies three stages of Christian spiritual development resulting in acceptance of grace: purgative, illuminative, and unitive. In all three stages,

As the individual is purified, so is the quality of his or her service; as the service is purified, so is the individual.

*Duality
becomes
resolved as
purification
occurs.*

purification plays a major role. In the purgation stage, disciples strive to emulate Christ in thought and action by removing the obstacles to seeing him in every other person. Purification occurs as the person confronts again and again the discrepancy between personal action and the model set forth in the Sermon on the Mount. As they succeed in this level of purification, they move into the illuminative stage becoming more aware of the obstacles placed in the way of loving God. The loving call to Christ and the gifts of the Holy Spirit coexist with the purging of deeply rooted and repressed conflicts. Duality becomes resolved as purification occurs. In the unitive stage, the disciple becomes absorbed in the quiet joy and union with God. There are also periods of further purification, "dark nights," during which God seems totally absent. The passing of these tests of purity and faith result in an experience of total peace and stillness.

SERVICE AS DEVOTION

Any religion followed to its highest expression, leads to transcendent experience: union with the Absolute. Once integration of all aspects of being takes place, personal psychology rests in God. This is the experience of the mystic. A necessary ingredient of that experience is devotion, the deep, sweet experience of being in love with the Absolute. From the depths of devotion come the songs of ecstasy from the saints, the psalmists, and the poets. In a single moment of mystical union, Uvanuk, a Netisilik Eskimo woman, received a song. When she sang it, she was able to heal others.

> *The great sea has set me in motion,*
> *set me adrift,*
> *moving me like a weed in a river.*

The sky and the strong wind
have moved the spirit inside me
till I am carried away
trembling with joy.

A mystic experiences service and devotion to the Absolute as the same. The presence of God permeates the inner being and this presence extends to all thought and action in daily life. Service becomes an altar of devotion. The presence alone of an individual of such purity, humility, and innocence serves others.

Mysticism is the most advanced level of spiritual development on the path of the soul's evolution. Mysticism includes the possibility of attaining union with the Divine and the means of attaining that union. While mysticism expresses through the religion of the individual mystic, it also transcends religious differences. Metaphorically, all mystics speak the same language. As a consequence, they form an international spiritual network that has the potential for providing the world with its greatest hope for peace and community.

Far from being withdrawn from the world, mystics are ordinary people who are active in the world through a state of transcendent being. The mystic's life is one of dedication to God while being engaged in work, relationships, and service. Evelyn Underhill, writer and teacher of Christian spirituality, defined three elements characterizing mysticism. First, mysticism is an approach to life that is practical and transformative rather than theoretical. Second, absorption in God dominates the mystic's path; the mystic and the path are one. Third, the mystic's life centers on doing the will of God out of love; service in the world is service to God.

The mystic's life is one of dedication to God while being engaged in work, relationships, and service.

SYNTHESIS

A common thread weaves itself throughout the teachings of

all religions: one's inner call to God is the call to live a life of love through service. Whether service is practiced as duty, charity, purification, or devotion, the call to service expresses the desire to love through action. As we explore the dimensions of service, we discover service *as* life rather than as something we *do* in life; we discover that everything we do is service.

For example, when we experience the pleasure of eating an ice cream cone, we allow a certain energy of delight to flow. The greater our joy and delight in our eating, the more energy flows through us, encouraging those around us to take more joy in their eating. Even in solitude this energy of delight flows from us, touching those we do not see. Physicists, mathematicians, biologists, mystics, and poets increasingly share the belief that the universe is a web of interrelated systems driven by energy. Very possibly the flutter of the butterfly in China contributes to the hurricane in Mexico, and the expression of delight or distaste at a dinner table in Peru affects someone in Alaska. Nothing happens that is inconsequential; everything is energy, everything is service.

The truth of the pervasiveness of service requires that we work diligently to chisel away all that stands between us and our soul's full expression. This involves the willingness to examine the shadow, the part of ourselves from which we spend much of our lives hiding. Working with the shadow exposes our natural state of grace; in a sense, this effort is all it takes to lift a finger to touch God. When we lift a finger and touch God, we weave our love throughout the world as service.

Working with the shadow exposes our natural state of grace; in a sense, this effort is all it takes to lift a finger to touch God. When we lift a finger and touch God, we weave our love throughout the world as service.

CHAPTER FOUR

The Shadow of Service

After many years as a recovering alcoholic and participant in two twelve-step programs, Lila agreed to be a twelve-step sponsor for Phyllis. Phyllis' substance abuse had left her homeless and out of work. Lila proceeded to help Phyllis in every way she could. She offered her room and board in her own home and supported her in finding a job by helping her select the proper clothes, typing her resume, and driving her to interviews. She accompanied Phyllis to twelve-step meetings and provided an immediate presence whenever Phyllis had a crisis. Lila felt fulfilled, and Phyllis began getting her life in order.

One day, about six months into their relationship, during a discussion of Phyllis' progress, Phyllis suddenly blew up at Lila, calling her "manipulative, controlling, and poisonous." Lila was devastated. Only after intense self-examination was she able to admit that her own need to be nurtured and affirmed motivated her service. By trying to "fix" Phyllis, she had projected her loneliness and her lack of self-love, self-appreciation, and self-worth onto her. As long as Phyllis accepted the projection, Lila felt fulfilled—her needs were met.

MEETING THE SHADOW OF SERVICE

When we meet and own our shadow of service, the pure light of the soul pours through us spontaneously and contains no self-reference, using intuition to dispel illusions. The convergence of our inner journey with our outer one leads to the discovery of the soul's unique destiny. Gradually, we move from being self-centered to being centered on humanity.

The shadow brings unfulfilled potentials to our awareness. As we claim our shadow, the psychic energy once held in the disowned parts of ourselves becomes available for our evolution, our creativity, and our service. Without fear and guilt, we can willingly examine our hidden motives for service, asking whether we are serving to satisfy our need for power, fame, affection, or validation. We witness our tendencies to make ourselves or others superior to the rest of humanity. We acknowledge the many ways our personality distorts the purity of our giving. Our willingness to meet our shadow allows us to consciously make another choice.

When someone is in distress, we serve by responding, with their permission, to relieve their suffering to the fullest extent possible and with a commitment for the highest good for all concerned. To use a common metaphor, this action "gives the hungry fish to eat." Then, as the story goes, we encourage self-responsibility by teaching them to fish. True Service adds one more step. True Service teaches people to understand how to create, maintain, and participate in a healthy environment in which both they and the fish can thrive as a part of nature as a whole. This additional step offers those we serve the gift of choice and with it the freedom of unlimited possibilities.

Being committed to our own growth means being committed to meeting our shadow. The reward of this commitment occurs

As we claim our shadow, the psychic energy once held in the disowned parts of ourselves becomes available for our evolution, our creativity, and our service.

when True Service begins to express through us. Then gratitude overwhelms us for the many learning opportunities provided by the shadow.

THE SHADOW
AND ITS MOTIVATION TO SERVE

As long as the shadow remains hidden, we live in the fetid swamp of blocked energy. As we take responsibility for the shadow, the Life Force flows from the spring of well-being.

The shadow holds the neglected, undeveloped, unlived, negative, and destructive aspects of our psyches. It also contains shameful and unacceptable desires and emotions. The shadow operates like a veil over the soul, virtually overshadowing the energy of the higher truth of who we are and affecting the purity of the soul's expression. Until we learn to observe ourselves with detachment, we remain largely unaware of our inner motivations and the impact we have on others. Unconscious motivations, often accompanied by neglect of our own physical, mental, and spiritual health, contaminate our service. In the story of Lila and Phyllis, Phyllis sensed Lila's hidden motivations. The more Lila did for her, the more Phyllis felt imposed upon. She then projected her feelings of powerlessness onto Lila in rage.

According to Carl Jung, the shadow is the part of the psyche that resides in the personal unconscious. In literature, the shadow symbolizes the hidden past and the primitive and inferior parts of the self. We can think of the shadow as creating the blocks to the flow of the Life Force. As long as the shadow remains hidden, we live in the fetid swamp of blocked energy. As we take responsibility for the shadow, the Life Force flows from the spring of well-being.

Jungian analyst Robert Johnson sees the shadow as our psyche's attempt to hide the duality of both dark and light. Not only do we refuse our negative traits, we also may refuse our finer qualities. Because the shadow contains potential for growth and nobility, Jung described it as 90 percent gold. Although it seems absurd, the shadow's gold often frightens us more than its darkness. We may even project our finer qualities outward, making other people into heroes or beings with qualities superior to and unattainable for ourselves. We thereby let others carry our personal potential for positive and constructive talents and qualities.

Johnson uses the symbol of a seesaw to describe the two sides of the personality. The visible and desirable characteristics sit on one side of the seesaw and the hidden, forbidden characteristics on the other. When we indulge the characteristics of either side, we subject the psyche to extreme stress. The stress causes us to lose our balance and flip into the opposite behavior. For example, Lila focused totally on being "the good person who sacrifices by helping others." Her shadow evidenced itself in the opposite behavior, her pride for her sacrifice. Lila displayed this by being sure everyone knew how helpless Phyllis would have been without her.

As we progress toward wholeness, we are challenged to balance the light and the dark by focusing our attention on the center of the seesaw. We experience balance by standing in the middle and honoring the truth of both sides. We no longer oppose our duality. Rather, we own our shadow and embrace the paradox of polarity. Instead of experiencing the tension of an either/or, all-or-none world, we experience a world beyond opposites.

"To transform opposition into paradox," says Johnson, "is to allow both sides of an issue, both pairs of opposites, to exist in equal dignity and worth. If I can stay with my conflicting impulses long enough, the two opposing forces will teach each other something and produce an insight that serves them both." Johnson uses the term "creative synthesis" to describe the shift in energy accompanying the balancing of light and dark. Creative synthsisis

Creative synthesis occurs when our self-knowledge rises to the level of spiritual wisdom, beyond the polarities of psychological and physical realities.

*The quality
and integrity of
our service
directly reflect
our willingness to
be conscious of
and responsible
for our
inner attitudes
and beliefs
toward those
we serve and
toward ourselves
as servers.*

occurs when our self-knowledge rises to the level of spiritual wisdom, beyond the polarities of psychological and physical realities. We may experience such a synthesis as a transcendent moment, a spiritual insight, or a gift of grace. Frequently the experience manifests in a visible change in our personality natures. For example, when Lila accepted the motivations of her shadow and balanced them with her generosity, kindness, and willingness to serve, she noticeably changed. Once perceived as distant, she became gentle, humble, and open to her own and others' mistakes. Unless we take responsibility for the shadow, we burden others and lose the opportunity for creative synthesis.

The energy of the shadow is also visible in how we receive service. When we disown receiving and only give, we set up a polarity in the psyche that leads to a need to control both giving and receiving. Lila obviously defended herself against receiving anything from Phyllis. She confined her receiving to having her needs met through her giving. She denied Phyllis the joy of giving, confining her to a role that was thereby less than human. Only giving is like breathing out and never breathing in. This leads to burnout. Only receiving is like breathing in and holding one's breath. This leads to lifelessness. True Service is alive, vital, natural, and joyous. True Service breathes in, breathes out, and recognizes the sacred moment of silence between breaths.

The shadow presents a further paradox. Light cannot exist without darkness; therefore, the more light-filled our conscious personality becomes, the more shadow we have. Johnson writes that "to make light is to make shadow; one cannot exist without the other." As a result, the more enlightened we are, the more vigilant we must be of our shadow side.

The quality and integrity of our service directly reflect our willingness to be conscious of and responsible for our inner attitudes and beliefs toward those we serve and toward ourselves as servers. Our motivation to serve impacts those we serve and those who serve us. A potential exists for both harm and good. A nurse tells this story:

> I was working the evening shift in the hospital; we were very busy. An old Native American man kept ringing his bell. His legs ached and he wanted a massage. I told him repeatedly that I was busy, that there were emergencies. He persisted until I went to massage his legs.
>
> I was a little angry with him for not understanding the stress of my job. I said to myself, "I'll pretend I'm massaging Christ's legs; I'll make it an act of service." So I began to massage his legs. He lay still, not grateful, but openly receptive. He knew he fully deserved my attention. Slowly, powerfully, an immense sense of love, renewal, and vitality flowed through every cell of my body. I realized I *was* massaging the legs of Christ.
>
> This dear grandfather had called me into his room to give me this gift of divine awareness. And I had thought he wanted something from me.

Service without attention to the quality and health of our inner life leads to inertia, depression, resentment, poverty of spirit, and lifeless service.

The level at which the grandfather received and gave back and his total acceptance transformed the nurse's anger and resistance. The value and integrity of our work depend upon the quality of our intent and our willingness to shift from a closed to an open heart.

Service without attention to the quality and health of our inner life leads to inertia, depression, resentment, poverty of spirit, and lifeless service. When we do not honor the shadow, we go

*When we do
not honor
the shadow,
we go forth
like the thrust
of a wave car-
ried along by
the power of
hidden
undercurrents.*

forth like the thrust of a wave carried along by the power of hidden undercurrents. These undercurrents, operating as projection, denial, or neglect, represent unconscious shadow challenges to the quality of our inner lives and therefore to the quality of our service. Most of us contaminate our service in each of these ways some of the time. The degree to which we do so depends on our level of awareness.

Coming to terms with the shadow is the work of the soul's evolution. Self-growth and serving others are inseparable and complementary human activities. We integrate and ground the learning of our personal inner healing work by applying it in service in our daily lives. In turn, our service reinforces our self-knowledge and strengthens our inner healing. Like an infinity sign, the energy of giving continually flows into the energy of receiving and back again.

THE SHADOW PROJECTED

Service can be a projection of our fear or guilt rather than an act of true compassion. We might give up our seat on the bus out of fear of violence or perform some service at work because we fear losing our job. Awareness of our own advantages might motivate us to serve those we perceive as unfortunate so that we can assuage our feelings of guilt and worthlessness.

Mark, a corporate executive who admits to many personal insecurities about his value and competence, helps regularly in the kitchen at a homeless shelter. He explains, "I feel so guilty that I have so much and they have so little. Who am I to have so many work opportunities and a comfortable life? I feel better when I help these poor people." Mark's service is an attempt to satisfy his need to be innocent and guilt-free.

Projection is the process by which we impose our shadow on someone or something outside ourselves. Through projection, we give away those qualities, positive and negative, that we do not want to accept in ourselves. When we project, we impose our will on someone or something else by imposing our beliefs and ideas. By imposing our will, we disempower the recipient while serving our own needs. Rather than giving, we take.

One day I received a call from a woman frantic with concern for a friend with AIDS. "He won't listen to me!" she complained. "There are so many things he could do to get well and he won't do them. How can his friends help him when he won't let himself be helped?"

The woman thought she was being helpful and supportive by showering her friend with tapes, books, and a myriad of holistic health alternatives. She was desperate for her friend to accept the approach she herself would use if she had a life-threatening illness. In her own life, she was not practicing the preventative aspects of the approach to health that she herself supported. As a result, she projected her need to be self-responsible onto her friend. She was giving the wrong thing in the wrong amount at the wrong time and for the wrong reason.

We know we have accepted a projection by our emotional response to what is happening. The person to whom we throw a projection only catches it if the projected image matches an image the recipient holds in his or her own shadow. For example, when Lila projected onto Phyllis a belief in Phyllis' powerlessness, Phyllis reacted because she also believed she was powerless. If she had felt centered in her inner power, she would not have needed to react in self-defense and might not even have noticed Lila's projection. Whenever we feel ourselves throw or catch a projection, we have shadow issues to address.

Through projection, we give away those qualities, positive and negative, that we do not want to accept in ourselves.

*Shadow
tendencies of
individuals blend
together to form
a group
or collective
shadow.*

Shadow tendencies of individuals blend together to form a group or collective shadow. Service groups and organizations have different styles for exhibiting their collective shadow energy depending upon the nature of their shadow tendencies. For example, if several persons in a group feel powerless because they have disowned their self-worth, they may collectively project their authority issues onto the leader. As a group, they may challenge the leader's role and knowledge. The group may, instead, disown their potential for leadership and project the total burden of responsibility for the organization onto the leader. In the latter instance, the group is then likely to view the leader as superior, flawless, and unreachable. At the same time the group is disowning its leadership potential, the leader may be projecting his or her fears about leadership onto the group through excessive control or need for positive feedback. The collective shadow of members of a group always overlaps the leader's shadow.

As a nation, one way we project our collective shadow onto service is through reductionism, reducing an integrated system to fragmented parts. The universe is composed of interactive and interconnected systems: solar systems, ecosystems, governments, businesses, families, bodies, and so forth. Nothing exists in isolation; each system affects other systems and each part of a system affects the whole and *vice versa*. A reductionistic view fails to recognize the systemic nature of things and results in categorization and dualistic thinking. When we disown our wholeness, we see a fragmented world. When we disown a part of ourselves, we project that part outward. One reason we project our fragmented reality onto the world is to reduce things to manageable pieces. We think, "Now I am doing service, now I am not," or, "That is service, this is not." Reductionistic thinking pervades the helping professions as well as the fields of business, education, and industry. It is highly evi-

dent in the field of medicine where physicians specialize in diag-
nosing and treating parts of the body rather than the body as a
whole system.

POWER AND FAME

Service can become a field for harvesting power and fame.
The seeds of ambition, hidden and dormant in the server, can
find fertile ground in acts of helping. Whether as a leader of a
service organization or a volunteer, a helpful neighbor, or an in-
charge secretary, one can use service as a way to feel personally
powerful and to receive rewards and recognition. An attitude of
"I am important because I can give something special that people
need and do not have" expresses a desire for power and fame.
Sustaining this attitude over time leads eventually to misalignment of the head and heart. Intellect and knowledge become
separated from wisdom and compassion. The use of the skillful
will to develop skill and competency becomes disconnected from
the use of the good will for serving the good of humanity. Like the
characters in Douglass Wallop's *Damn Yankees*, we can sell our
souls for power and fame.

Service provides a stage to act out apparent power in order to
receive outside validation of personal significance. True power is
inner strength. We discover our inner strength when we are tolerant of our weaknesses, not when we avoid them. By patiently
addressing the feelings arising from loss of a job, illness, depression, or death of a loved one, we strengthen ourselves. Power
pours in when we persevere with the inner healing process and
honor our expanding self-knowledge and growth. True power
comes from an open heart.

When we disown our true power by projecting it and believing it lies outside ourselves, we repress the Life Force and feel

*When we disown
our wholeness,
we see
a fragmented
world.*

*True power is
inner strength.
We discover our
inner strength
when we are
tolerant of our
weaknesses, not
when we
avoid them.*

powerless and insecure. With our true power hidden, we rely on creating apparent power, the illusion of power, in a desperate attempt to regain wholeness and to survive physically or psychologically. Out of insecurity, we act strong, confident, and in control, when inwardly we feel powerless and therefore victimized. As a result, we polarize the world into victims and victimizers and project this belief onto those we serve. To be saviors, we must see others as helpless and in need of saving.

Heather shared that her parents received numerous awards for their contributions and leadership of many charitable organizations, community projects, and boards. The community considered them leaders of innovative change. By contrast, at home they were both active alcoholics who expressed their insecurities and lack of true power by unleashing their inner torment on their five children through psychological and physical abuse.

Heather's parents failed to recognize the shadow side of their psyches and failed to integrate their physical, social, and emotional selves. They unconsciously believed in their own powerlessness, manifesting this belief in their alcoholism, abusiveness, and in their conspiracy to hide their behaviors. They disowned their true power and expressed apparent power as altruistic and responsible citizens.

As illustrated in this story, the potential for misuse of power lies within each person rather than within a role or setting. The misuse of power may appear in any relationship in which one person is perceived to have more power than another.

Motivations of power or fame also make us vulnerable to projecting our hidden fears and desires about the body. Stories abound of counselors who sexually misuse patients, physicians who sell and use drugs, and religious leaders who extort funds to engage in lavish life-styles. Anyone serving in a position of trust and authority is susceptible to using intellectual or spiritual knowledge to manipulate others in order to satisfy desire for power and fame. Those who do this must psychically deny or split off their physical natures, for example, by denying sexual passion, aging, and infirmity. A polarized view of the body as either flesh or spirit, sinful or innocent, animal or godlike, selfish or altruistic, characterizes this split. The disowned polarity gathers an all-consuming energy and strives to balance itself in extreme ways. A disowned body results in guilt and shame about bodily functions and leads to addictive and abusive behaviors. These may include substance abuse, eating disorders, gambling, sexual addiction, physical and sexual abuse, inappropriate sexual behavior, and financial excess and irresponsibility.

PRIDE

Whether pride manifests covertly or overtly, the desire for recognition as "the one most responsible for the good that happens in the lives of others" motivates the prideful server. Such a server desires approval and recognition in the form of awards and special favors. When motivated by pride, we want others to believe that we are more giving than most and that what we give is uniquely valuable and important. Unless we receive sufficient appreciation for ourselves or our cause, we lose interest in giving and move on to where we feel our worth will be acknowledged.

We can most easily identify pride when it manifests overtly as a sales pitch for the "right way." Pride motivates individuals and groups who believe their approach is the only approach. They strive to "sell" their "product" because they believe they know what people need and that their services are both superior and indispensable.

Competition, jealousy, and rigidity about what is right and

Anyone serving in a position of trust and authority is susceptible to using intellectual or spiritual knowledge to manipulate others in order to satisfy desire for power and fame.

wrong usually accompany overt pride. Covert pride is an even more insidious and pervasive means of projection. Under the guise of humility and love, covert pride manifests as false humility, martyrdom, and competition.

Pride can cause us to engage in comparison in order to assure ourselves of our own worth and ability.

False humility is another aspect of pride in which a desire for praise and recognition manifests as denial of that desire and as disparagement of our gifts and talents. When we engage in false humility we discount and negate the value of our giving. We are inauthentic, saying the opposite of what we believe and want. Anyone working with or being served by us senses our inauthenticity and feels patronized. False humility tends to evoke guilt in others, and guilt is a powerful tool for manipulation and victimization.

Because pride arises from a need to feel superior, a prideful server necessarily victimizes those served to some degree. Whenever we victimize someone else, we do so because of our own feelings of being a victim. As a result, from false humility it is a short step to martyrdom. Martyrs give to get. As martyrs, when we do not get what we want, we feel victimized by the persons to whom we have given and want to punish them. Our self-pity takes the form of "poor me." We call attention to our own helpfulness and to the lack of appreciation expressed by those we have helped. Then, to perpetuate the cycle, we continue to offer help to the same people who, in turn, feel guilty, betrayed, emotionally manipulated, and abused.

Pride can cause us to engage in comparison in order to assure ourselves of our own worth and ability. Comparison leads to competition and jealousy, behaviors based on a belief that love, recognition, success, and talent are scarce commodities that we lack. We compete for this limited supply by making others wrong, sometimes to the point of violating personal and professional standards.

Unhealthy competition especially evidences as a shadow issue in the world of political and social activism. Many activists enjoy conflict for the sake of fighting a good fight. In the joy of the fray, they often fixate on a point of view, expect blind loyalty, and are callous about the consequences of their actions. Fueled with the energy of rage and the importance and validity of the cause, activists compete aggressively against those with opposing views. If pride takes over, activists may fall in love with, and even obsess on, an issue. The many things to fight for, participate in, and save can dominate their lives. They may also focus on keeping alive the memories of wrongdoing. The urgency and emotion of causes are usually associated with adolescence when individuals are particularly prone to polarized views of the world. Activists of any age can use a cause as a focus of their rage about a personal hurt and to avoid inner work.

Competitive pride also causes comparison of the relative importance of forms of service. People commonly view service to the dying, the disabled, the homeless, or those in crisis or disaster situations as more important than mowing a neighbor's lawn or opening a door for someone. Following the 1995 federal building bombing in Oklahoma City, a resident observed people competing for certain roles. They considered leading crisis support groups or organizing memorials as more prestigious and valuable than listening to another's experience or taking someone's child to school. The prideful categorization of roles, especially in a time of great tragedy, reinforces feelings of victimization and helplessness among those served.

When out of pride we communicate an air of superiority by conveying that we have our lives together when we do not, those being served feel patronized, belittled, and betrayed. It is natural for those receiving service to question the humanity of those who

When out of pride we communicate an air of superiority by conveying that we have our lives together when we do not, those being served feel patronized, belittled, and betrayed.

serve them.

Irene noted that Caucasians often came to the reservation where she worked because they wanted to "help the Indians." The Native Americans frequently blocked the efforts of these people both overtly and covertly. Many individuals told Irene that they did not understand why white people could not leave them alone to take care of themselves, even if they did it poorly. Inwardly they seemed to ask, "Who are these people, what are they doing here, and why do they keep returning?"

Trustworthy servers are authentic and whole human beings who share their confusions and mistakes, joys and accomplishments.

Trustworthy servers are authentic and whole human beings who share their confusions and mistakes, joys and accomplishments. We live in a world of shared humanity with multiple opportunities to learn and grow. When we share our whole selves, we share authentically. We communicate our genuineness and do not pretend we are something we are not.

When we feel unappreciated or self-righteous, we have an opportunity to explore our true motives for serving. We use that opportunity to ask ourselves if we are giving to get or giving to share our genuine care for others. We explore the feeling of defeat that arises when a victory is not rewarded or an idealistic dream is not realized. Pride in giving closes the heart and separates the giver from those served.

SENTIMENT

When we serve from sentiment, we use feelings and emotions as the basis for our thoughts, opinions, judgements, attitudes, and actions. We view the world and our interactions with others through the lens of emotion. Our emotions color our perceptions and decisions. Intense feelings, inspired by beauty, love, sorrow, and pain and expressed with deep passion, can frighten others. As a result, we may learn to hold back the feelings some of the time, usually at the risk of having them erupt with even greater force at another time.

Sentiment focuses on relationships, love, and loss. It arises from experiences of great suffering and results in a need to feel special. When motivated by sentiment, we often assume that others experience the same intense suffering and emotion as we do. As a result, we seek validation of our emotions from those we serve or serve with, exploiting them to meet our emotional needs.

When we are out of touch with the True Self, our emotional boundaries lack clarity. We take on others' moods and are empathic to their pain. We may be too sensitive to criticism, hurt at the tiniest slight, and feel that something is wrong or missing in our lives. We serve the world of effects. The pain and suffering of others remind us of our own; we strive to eliminate our personal distress and discomfort by relieving theirs and taking on their responsibilities. By focusing on alleviating others' suffering, we risk preventing them from learning lessons necessary for the evolution of their souls.

By focusing on alleviating others' suffering, we risk preventing them from learning lessons necessary for the evolution of their souls.

I once observed a good example of the importance of allowing others to take responsibility for their own situations rather than reacting from sentiment. The city bus I was riding stopped to pick up a woman on crutches. Almost instantaneously, several people at the front of the bus jumped up to help her climb the steps. Immediately she cried out, "Leave me alone! I want to get on this bus *myself!*" The helpers sat down meekly, and we all waited while she ascended the steps and took her seat.

Personally overwhelmed by this woman's struggles, the willing helpers unconsciously thought, "I would hate to be disabled and dependent." They then projected their fear onto her and jumped to help. They assumed they were being empathic, but true empathy demands that we *know* what the other person feels before we determine that we can share the feeling. Obviously this woman did not see herself as helpless and knew that people served her best by being empathic to her inner strength and physical independence.

By overlooking the fact that those we serve have different needs and concerns than ourselves, we also deny our own needs. To validate our perceived perception of their needs, we deny ourselves in order to please and meet their personality demands. For example, out of sentiment, the parents of a child with severe disabilities might exhaust themselves doing everything for the child rather than pushing the child to explore her own potential, however limited.

ATTACHMENT

There are four primary ways that attachment affects the quality of service. Three of these are: attachment to the form of service, to the outcome of service, and/or to the people served. In the fourth, we encourage those we serve to be attached to us. Attachment arises from the belief that something outside ourselves is essential to our physical, emotional, or mental well-being. Attachment causes us to grasp and hang on to a relationship, concept, or material possession in the belief that our life depends on its presence. Pride taints our attachments when we engage in competition and comparison related to the superior value of what we do, the results we obtain, whom we serve, and how needed we are. Such an attitude is arrogant and proud and arises from a heart closed to opportunities to learn compassion. Attachment destroys the spirit of life by reinforcing the illusion that we are separate from one another rather than part of an interdependent system.

Attachment destroys the spirit of life by reinforcing the illusion that we are separate from one another rather than part of an interdependent system.

ATTACHMENT TO FORM

When attached to a form of service, we seek validation of our self-worth from the roles and activities through which we serve. Our motivation to serve is conditional, dependent on how our service is perceived by others and how much it enhances our self-image.

A materialistic society such as ours is a manifestation of attachment to form. We are not simply attached to people, objects, or money; we are attached to the form of what we call success and what we call service. These attachments reflect a belief that service is a separate activity rather than a natural and integrated part of our lives individually and communally.

Our true heroes are those who in their lifetimes inspire others through their selfless service.

I once met a man who insisted that he did not participate in service. Yet when I asked him if he was a father, he said yes. He admitted that he had never thought of fatherhood as service; he thought service only meant helping the unfortunate. Even when we view parenting as service, however, we can be attached to the form of our role. One father may become attached to serving his children as a provider and playmate and avoid the roles of teacher, disciplinarian, and nurturer. Another may do just the opposite.

Nonattachment is a precept of the monastic traditions of most religions, but some people in secular occupations have also demonstrated it. Our true heroes are those who in their lifetimes inspire others through their selfless service. Abi 'l-Khayr wrote, "The true saint goes in and out amongst the people and eats and sleeps with them and buys and sells in the market and marries and takes part in social intercourse, and never forgets God for a single moment." A few well-known people who have lived their life in this way are the Carmelite Brother Lawrence, the Sufi poet Rumi, the English nurse Florence Nightingale, the German physician

Albert Schweitzer, the Native American elder Twylah Nitsch, and the Swedish statesman Dag Hammarskjöld.

ATTACHMENT TO OUTCOME

Attached to outcome, we believe our well-being is dependent on the product of our service. We measure our success by whether or not we achieved a specific product. For example, if an environmentalist is attached to the outcome of her campaign to stop the clear-cutting of forests, she may feel she has personally failed if her campaign is unsuccessful.

Attachment to outcome invariably leads to burnout, a state of physical and mental exhaustion. When we continually expend our energies in pursuit of a specific end result, we deny ourselves the joy and replenishment that comes from participating fully in the process. We may rush past potentially meaningful relationships, ignore opportunities, and even hurt our cause by being totally outcome focused. Martin Luther King, Jr., said, "Whatever we say or think, this is arduous duty, doing this kind of work: to live out one's idealism brings with it hazards."

Sometimes the outcome we seek is a specific response from those we serve. When Carol offered to tutor seven-year-old Kelly, she expected to make a dramatic difference in Kelly's life and to receive his eternal gratitude. Kelly resisted being tutored by being inattentive and sometimes belligerent. Carol persisted in trying to break through his resistance, but nothing changed. After each session, she felt so exhausted she considered resigning. Finally, in desperation, Carol quit resisting Kelly's resistance and adjusted her expectations to match his emotional needs. Kelly became cooperative, and Carol felt energized and inspired by the sessions.

At other times, the outcome we seek is the physical and emotional exultation that results from certain kinds of achievements. Research indicates that helping others actually increases endorphin levels, creating a natural "high," lowering stress, and enhancing feelings of well-being. While this "high" reinforces a positive behavior, its shadow side is that one can become emotionally and physiologically addicted to the experience. An addiction is the attachment to the outcome of a given behavior. Meeting the needs of the addiction takes precedence over the needs of anyone or anything else. Addiction to a physical high easily becomes linked with other things perceived as positive outcomes of service, such as respect, praise, and the validation of the value of one's work.

One woman whose work earned her a place on the lecture and conference circuit shared that during and after presentations she felt enervated and totally alive. She loved sharing her life's work with eager listeners and felt that her contribution really counted. She felt that she was finally being rewarded for her years of hard, and sometimes lonely, work. While life on the circuit was glamorous and rewarding, life between presentations began to feel dull and unfulfilling. As a result, she accepted more and more invitations. Her children complained of her absences, her husband felt burdened and used, and she could not maintain the quality of the very work that had merited the speaking engagements. Soon she became physically ill and emotionally exhausted. She then realized she had become addicted to attention and praise to the point that she had been willing to give up everything else in her life. Similarly, people who regularly volunteer in emergency and disaster situations may be attached to the exhilaration of being heroes in times of need.

ATTACHMENT TO THOSE WE SERVE

When we are attached to those we serve, we cross physical

An addiction is the attachment to the outcome of a given behavior.

Once we disentangle ourselves from feelings and responsibilities that do not belong to us, we can allow others to be accountable for their own choices.

and emotional boundaries. We risk assuming responsibility for the feelings and experiences of others, and we risk becoming addicted to our service. We can become attached to those we serve in marriage, family, personal, work, and professional or social settings.

In his book *Boundaries and Relationships*, psychiatrist Charles Whitfield explains that taking on another's responsibility is an attempt to gain acceptance and love. This tendency, the result of poorly defined boundaries, can lead to attempts to change, rescue, or fix others. Whitfield writes that as we become aware of our True Self, we are able to discern "what is mine and what is not mine." We learn to tell the difference between our own needs, feelings, and projections and those of others. This clarity about ourselves enables us to make choices harmonious with the beliefs, attitudes, and actions of our True Self. Once we disentangle ourselves from feelings and responsibilities that do not belong to us, we can allow others to be accountable for their own choices.

Attachment issues are common in intimate relationships, such as in marriage and other partnerships. After several years of marriage, Mary puzzled over her extreme attachment to being responsible for her husband Dan's thoughts and behavior. It was as though she herself thought his shadow thoughts and performed his irresponsible acts. Mary readily acknowledged that her greatest fear in her marriage was that Dan would betray and therefore abandon her, physically, emotionally, and spiritually. Her fear of abandonment caused her to distrust Dan. She exhibited this by continually criticizing and correcting him. She desperately wanted him to change. After doing extensive inner work, Mary observed that her fear of abandonment had prevented her from identifying and claiming her feelings, beliefs, dreams, and preferences. She saw that she was the abandoner by having abandoned her True Self.

As a result of her insight, a healing occurred in the marriage, and Mary began allowing Dan to be responsible for his own choices and behavior. In time, Mary recognized that her marriage relationship could be one in which each party supported and served the other.

As members of families, we exhibit attachment issues anytime we attempt to help a situation by taking on the responsibility of another member's feelings and behavior. By assuming this responsibility, we hope the person will change his or her behavior and the problem will disappear. This is usually part of a long established pattern of victim and rescuer. When we rescue the victim, we can claim to be a good parent, child, or sibling. This in turn assuages any guilt we hold about these relationships. On the other hand, rescuer and victim may both be attached to the problem and not want it solved. We can define ourselves by the role we play in a problem to such an extent that we may unconsciously fear that solving the problem may threaten our very existence. We are attached to the *status quo* and fear the results of change.

Whether within the family or within society, whenever we rely on a person, group of people, or a cause as the source and supply of our life energy, we exhibit attachment to those we serve. In such cases we act on the belief that the presence of someone or something outside ourselves, like a cause or a role, is what gives life meaning and purpose. Attached to the sense of well-being we receive from those we serve or from a cause we espouse, we lose sight of the True Self as the only source of well-being. We contract around the Life Force. We give in order to take by using those we serve to replenish our energy. As a result, we become physically and mentally exhausted, and those we serve feel drained in our presence. The addiction to serving in this way is self-perpetuating because attachment precludes awareness of other possibilities.

As members of families, we exhibit attachment issues anytime we attempt to help a situation by taking on the responsibility of another member's feelings and behavior.

ENCOURAGING THOSE WE SERVE
TO ATTACH TO US

When we encourage others to meet their needs through us, we fail to support healthy boundaries and the True Self in them and in ourselves.

Ill-defined boundaries or an intense desire for power and fame may cause us to encourage those we serve to depend on our strength rather than their own. Out of our need to be loved and valued, we encourage those we help to depend on us for their physical, mental, emotional, or spiritual well-being. This is the mechanism underlying co-dependency by which one becomes an enabler. Those in the helping professions who serve in the hope of being rescued from emotional pain and members of co-dependent family systems are especially prone to this form of attachment. There is a reciprocal relationship between the presence of healthy boundaries and a sense of the True Self. One must have healthy boundaries and a sense of the True Self in order to support the same in others. When we encourage others to meet their needs through us, we fail to support healthy boundaries and the True Self in them and in ourselves. This action disempowers those we serve, whether they are family members, coworkers, or clients.

Sometimes, even without our encouragement, those we help can attach themselves to us. They do so out of a desire to possess and absorb our energy or out of an inability or unwillingness to accept responsibility for themselves. Individuals who feel like victims or martyrs and have difficulty receiving are especially prone to becoming attached to their helpers. Because they are unconscious of their connection to the True Self, such individuals have an insatiable need to fill their gaping wounds with the energy of others. At the same time they try to pull love from others, they push it away. Caught in this cycle of self-imposed victimization, they take and take and take and do not receive. For them, giving is a sacrifice, and they seek sacrifice from those who serve them. As a result, serving such people requires strong boundaries and total reliance on the True Self, rather than the personal self, as the source of energy.

THE SHADOW DENIED

Denial and projection are related and interdependent mechanisms. Power or fame, pride, sentiment, or attachment motivate the projected shadow. The denied shadow motivates us to evade service and disregard our need for competence.

Denial is an ego defense mechanism that suppresses unclaimed and undeveloped parts of ourselves, burying them in the unconscious. Each thing denied has a unique energetic configuration. The matching configuration of another event releases it from the unconscious. The release takes the form of a strong emotional reaction. Unless we understand the mechanism of denial and are willing to examine what is happening, we will project our denied fears and attributes onto our own bodies or onto others. For example, if one denies the part of oneself that neglects one's physical health, one may project irresponsibility onto physicians. One may project the fear of losing control of one's mental health by rejecting help offered by others. As a member of a group, one may claim that the group is emotionally unsafe when it is only oneself who feels this way. Still another example occurs when one claims others talk incessantly and never listen when that trait is one's own.

The denied shadow motivates us to evade service and disregard our need for competence.

EVASION

Evasion works in two ways: evasion of the natural urge to serve or the use of service to evade shadow issues. We evade our natural urge to serve primarily through inertia, a lack of initiative and energy, and a loss of interest and enthusiasm. Inertia is common among those who are self-occupied and/or emotionally depressed.

*We evade our
natural urge to
serve primarily
through inertia,
a lack of
initiative and
energy and
a loss of interest
and enthusiasm.*

We can preoccupy ourselves with our own development and limitations by wanting special treatment from God and others. Persistent self-preoccupation results in an implosion of energy and blockage of the Life Force. When stuck in inertia, we use our energy to deliberate over possible changes rather than to gather the inner resources to make them. We may ultimately lapse into depression, becoming totally self-occupied and paralyzed by fear and guilt. Although when trapped by inertia, extending a helping hand seems impossible, such movement often releases the paralysis.

Groups and organizations can also become self-occupied and evade service through inertia. Self-centered groups focus on their immediate survival at the exclusion of the needs of society. The group's energy does not move outside itself. Eventually, the energy of the group implodes, leading to loss of enthusiasm and participation. Such a group often denies its shadow, proclaiming the group to be uniquely harmonious. Self-absorption hides unidentified and unspoken conflict of interests among group members. The consequences of failing to have an outer focus stay submerged until some form of conflict erupts. The group will disband if members do not address their individual and collective shadow issues.

As an example, the Institute for Attitudinal Studies has two tenets: the participation in one's own healing process by choosing to see differently and the willingness to extend or share unconditionally that healing through service. Experience has taught us that we must vigilantly monitor the balance between these two tenets, between the inner and the outer directed aspects of the organization. If the organization becomes too self-focused, too oriented toward its own members' emotional needs, processes, and pain, its outer growth and quality of service to the community falters. The organization also falters if too much energy is extended outward so that the members feel unsupported and alone. In either instance, rebalancing requires examination of the discrepancy between the organization's stated purpose and the current reality. This entails examination of the collective shadow.

Inertia also appears in service in other circumstances. Service requires commitment and concentrated focus, and we may choose not to develop or use our will to sustain the effort. Service challenges us to learn and grow, and we may choose to withdraw or to ignore or deny the lessons. Inertia may encourage us to engage in "cosmetic service," service that makes us look good while being undemanding and unchallenging. Cosmetic service may take the form of giving only financially or serving on a committee that rarely meets.

American culture supports the evasion of direct service with tax laws that encourage end-of-year charitable donations. Although the donations certainly benefit the recipients, the giver can lose the inner benefits of true charity unless the motivation is deeper than financial self-service. Charitable organizations themselves encourage contributors to feel they should receive something tangible for their donation by offering premiums or public recognition. Some send unsolicited gifts to prospective donors, knowing that many people feel compelled to donate if they have received something.

The Life Force moves where its flow is unobstructed. In *The Path of Least Resistance*, Robert Fritz explains that we can create what we truly want by aligning how we live our lives with where we want to go in our lives. By creating this alignment, we use the path of least resistance to our advantage, and it takes us where we want to go.

Like workaholics, our very busyness allows us to avoid intimate relationships and self-inquiry. Because we are serving oth-

Inertia may encourage us to engage in "cosmetic service," service that makes us look good while being undemanding and unchallenging.

ers, however, we feel superior to those who overwork in less worthy occupations. We sacrifice the quality of our lives and our personal well-being, feeling our contribution is worth our suffering. We deny that we would rather suffer than face the realities of our mental state.

No matter how we use evasion in relation to service, the underlying motivations relate to denial of unrealized potential. We may disown our value and personal power, giving it to others to express. We may displace our fear and guilt about our perceived inadequacies by seeing ourselves as victims justified in self-preoccupation or by trying to prove our worth through over giving. Disowning our talents and capabilities reinforces both inertia and feelings of worthlessness.

To be competent servers, we need to acquire appropriate skills and to uphold professional or ethical standards.

INCOMPETENCE

Incompetence in service occurs when the heart and the head are misaligned. This occurs in one of two ways: the heart is open and the necessary skills are lacking, or the appropriate skills are present and the heart is closed. In his work on psychosynthesis, Roberto Assagioli defines this misalignment as an imbalance between love and will. To be competent servers, we need to acquire appropriate skills and to uphold professional or ethical standards.

For example, in reviewing its services, a nonprofit organization, which builds houses for low income families, discovered that the majority of its volunteers had an attitude of loving service but lacked construction skills. In construction, caring and compassion cannot substitute for the skills of carpenter, electrician, plumber, roofer, and painter. The organization had to find remedies for the volunteers' lack of skills. By contrast, a qualified and creative high school teacher volunteered to coordinate the Sunday School program at a church. Her lack of compassion for small children and for volunteer teachers who needed support negated her many creative skills and caused interpersonal conflicts.

We are self-responsible when we serve at the level of our ability and are aware of the balance between our skills and our compassion. In our desire to help, we may tend to take on tasks and responsibilities for which we are ill-prepared. Such well-intentioned, but misdirected, service can have potentially harmful consequences for ourselves and for those we serve. This form of incompetence occurs in all professions.

People in crisis are the most vulnerable to incompetent servers. The crisis tends to diminish discrimination and self-trust of their intuition. Especially in these situations, service providers are responsible for monitoring their own competence and, if necessary, referring the person elsewhere.

Healers and those in the helping professions are responsible for monitoring the effect of their intervention on the energy fields of their clients. Fragmentation of a person's energy field may occur if the helper moves the energy too quickly or in the wrong way. Competence in this area requires training in understanding the dynamics of the human psyche and in identifying the conditions necessary for its integration.

When we are not aware of the true needs of those we serve, we tend to assume that we know what would be helpful for the person.

When we are not aware of the true needs of those we serve, we tend to assume that we know what would be helpful for the person. We negate the individuality of those we serve by imposing our value system or personal experiences. As individuals, we differ in rate and stage of evolution, personality integration, life tasks, and personal history. It is therefore important to spend time and effort understanding someone before deciding how to help. This decision involves an intuitive awareness that what people believe they need can often be quite different from what best serves their welfare and spiritual progress.

When we do not successfully express our creativity, we risk projecting our unfulfilled potential onto others.

Incompetence is a form of denial to which people who engage in prideful competition or who serve out of sentiment are especially susceptible. When I first met Jack, he was working with the dying as a way of healing his own fears about death. His aura of fear impacted those he served, and he enhanced, rather than dissipated, his fear of death.

While in some cases our shadow energy may push us to do more than we are able, in other cases we might deny our true competence and resist doing all we can. If this is true, we need to examine our motives for continuing to serve in limited ways. When we do not successfully express our creativity, we risk projecting our unfulfilled potential onto others. We see ourselves as victims and believe the outer world is preventing us from expressing our talents. When we do not express our creativity or do not apply what we have learned, we risk dissipating our energy and undermining our psychological well-being. Our life circumstances—prejudice, political or economic suppression, or financial, family, or other stresses—may also thwart our expression of competence. The emergence of technology has also impacted how we express our competence and creativity.

The story of composer Felix Mendelssohn's sister, Fanny, illustrates the inhibition of creativity, the projection of unfulfilled potential, and finally the resolution of the conflict. Fanny Mendelssohn's musical talents were equal to those of her renowned brother. Because the standards of the day limited women's options, Fanny received little support for developing her creativity and expressing it publicly. Her biographer, Francoise Tillard, describes how Fanny withdrew into her brother's shadow and projected onto him "all her own hopes for the destiny that was denied her....Henceforth Felix lived the life she had no right to live." Fanny's projections of her unfulfilled potential often took the form of anger and depression. She eventually discovered, however, that she could express her creativity through private concerts. Sharing her musical gifts with others enhanced her sense of personal value and emotional well-being.

The organizations we serve as employees or volunteers have the same responsibilities as individuals for ensuring competence. Each organization is responsible for assessing its strengths and weaknesses, acquiring new skills, and properly preparing and training its members. A supportive environment encourages the individual to explore and expand talents and creativity. Such opportunities allow mastery of personal struggles and the growth of skills and wisdom. From such mastery and growth we can genuinely share with others. The organizations benefit from the joy, creativity, and ever-expanding skills of their workers. As English social reformer John Ruskin said, "When love and skill work together, expect a masterpiece." Unfortunately, some organizations offer such limited choices that those with both skill and compassion cannot give at their level of competence or explore their creativity.

Today we live in a technologically based, world economy with a service, rather than a manufacturing, orientation. As businesses expand and technology encroaches on human involvement, organizations increasingly recognize that the personal engagement of the worker is the basis for the quality of both product and service. The ultimate product of all organizations and businesses is service, and service to customers is dependent on creating positive relationships both within and without the organization. New constructs of organizational design are revolutionizing attitudes, communication, teamwork, and relationships in the workplace. Some constructs, like Peter Senge's learning organization design,

The ultimate product of all organizations and businesses is service, and service to customers is dependent on creating positive relationships both within and without the organization.

take into account the importance of individual and organizational self-inquiry, applying the knowledge of the individual's personal growth process to the organization.

The advances in organizational design have given rise to a new profession: organizational consultants. These consultants offer the service of helping organizations apply the new constructs. Such a business group, curious about our organization, visited the Institute. I asked them how their own organization applied the concepts of team building and shared vision. Several responded that although they taught others how to do it, their organization did not apply the knowledge. As a result, their own organization experienced discord and dissatisfaction. They, like many other consultants and experts, fail to see that competence depends on combining factual knowledge with application and experience.

We acquire competence as we are willing to learn from experience and to integrate factual knowledge with application.

With groups, as with individuals, there is a discrepancy between what is known to be effective and how the group or individual actually operates. The remedy for this discrepancy originates from the inside out. We acquire competence as we are willing to learn from experience and to integrate factual knowledge with application.

Groups with differing yet compatible missions often do not know how to be supportive in their communications. The busyness of each group combined with fear of survival often interferes with developing ways to cooperate rather than compete. One group can project its shadow onto that of another, resulting in miscommunication and conflict. As one example, a group can project incompetence onto another group and avoid looking at their own hidden limitations and inadequacies. In another example, a group may use pride to assure themselves that their purpose is more important to humanity than that of another group.

The family, one form of group, exhibits many incompetencies. Families typically neglect acquiring knowledge about parenting skills, sibling relationships, child development, and communication skills. Through generations, families perpetuate patterns of behavior that limit potentials and distort lives, not only within the family, but within other groups of which family members are a part. Organizations can easily become extensions of the dysfunction in their members' families.

There are two additional considerations regarding competence of servers. In certain situations, especially in times of crisis, we may need to serve in a way that goes beyond our competence. In such instances, we should not hesitate to serve in the best way we can. Second, excessive self-consciousness about our competence is detrimental. Self-consciousness leads to loss of spontaneity and obstructed intuition. We need to balance the awareness of self with the awareness of the other.

THE SHADOW NEGLECTED

Consistent attention to one's own physical, emotional, mental, and spiritual well-being is probably the greatest challenge for those who serve. Neglect occurs when we refuse to take responsibility for our projections and denials under the guise of focusing attention on the unending task of easing humanity's suffering. By focusing only on the needs of others, we sacrifice our own well-being and remain in the world of the suffering.

Some years ago, whenever I visited my spiritual teacher, she would ask, "And how are *you* doing, Susan?" At first, I responded with an automatic "fine." Later, when I contemplated her question, I had to admit I was neglecting my personal well-being.

A conflict between caring for others and caring for oneself reflects a belief in duality manifested in either/or thinking. We

Neglect occurs when we refuse to take responsibility for our projections and denials under the guise of focusing attention on the unending task of easing humanity's suffering.

Many people associate discipline with self-effort or rigidity, rather than as the means to get something we truly want. Actually, we can also be rigid in our passivity and lack of discipline.

believe we must either give to others and neglect caring for ourselves or care for ourselves and neglect others. Underlying this dualistic approach may be the belief that we do not deserve to take care of ourselves or that selflessness means doing what others ask or expect of us. As a result, we fail to develop the discipline of caring for ourselves, independent of others' expectations.

Our service is enthusiastic and easy when we are physically comfortable, emotionally calm, and mentally clear. Achieving comfort, calm, and clarity involves managing our time, setting our priorities, and being flexible. We say, "I don't have time to care for myself." In reality, we do not have time *not* to care for ourselves. Many people associate discipline with self-effort or rigidity, rather than as the means to get something we truly want. Actually, we can also be rigid in our passivity and lack of discipline.

To achieve balance and moderation, we look inside and align how we are living with what we want our lives to be. In this way, we will have the energy and integrity to honor and respect both ourselves and those we serve. Contemplating this question assists in setting priorities: "How can I care for family and work, or ask others to care for themselves, if I do not also care for myself?" To serve well, we need to prepare ourselves for service and to maintain our well-being. We do this by attending to our physical, emotional, mental, and spiritual health.

PHYSICAL HEALTH

The physical body is the instrument through which service expresses in the world. Vital and enthusiastic service is difficult if the body is physically ill, drained, uncomfortable, or in pain. When we fail to care for our physical health, our energy field becomes dense, impeding intuition, knowledge, and guidance from the True Self. When we cannot open ourselves to receive the infinite supply of higher energies, we use our limited personal reservoir of energy. As we deplete our energy supply, the physical body becomes strained and we experience fatigue or illness.

When Mother Teresa gathered her first group of nuns to serve the dying among the destitute of Calcutta, she required them to eat and live like those they served. Soon many of the nuns became ill and were unable to work. By neglecting themselves in the name of service, they negated their ability to serve. Mother Teresa quickly recognized that she and her nuns needed a balanced diet and adequate housing to carry out their work.

In the early 1970s I began leading workshops in personal healing. Often I became ill afterwards, suffering a severe sore throat that lasted several weeks. In my naivete I was unaware that leading these workshops required considerable energy. I gave away my personal energy when I focused attention on workshop attendees who were resistant or emotionally needy. At that time I was unaware of the impact of my diet and life-style on my energies. My physical body was not strong enough to hold the higher energies I was evoking. Once I recognized the relationship between the workshops and the illness, I asked my True Self for a healing dream.

When we cannot open ourselves to receive the infinite supply of higher energies, we use our limited personal reservoir of energy.

A group of people had driven my 1966 Volvo, and it had broken down. They have called AAA for help. I arrive at my car just as the mechanic looks under the hood. He says, "The battery of this car needs thirteen gallons of water." He fills the battery, and the people leave. I get in the Volvo and turn the key in the ignition. The car starts, and I drive away.

The dream revealed that my recurrent illness occurred because my body, my vehicle, became dehydrated during the workshops. Other people, the workshop participants, "drove" my vehicle until the battery, the conductor of energy, was depleted of water. Because my energy was low, I was vulnerable to assuming responsibility for the needs and behaviors of others. I needed water to recharge my energies. Once I increased my water intake before and during workshops, the sore throats ceased.

The physical, emotional, and mental aspects of health interrelate. Pure water and food, cleanliness, proper sleep, physical exercise, and ample fresh air and sunshine are essential to physical well-being. A regimen of energy-balancing exercises, body massages, and body-movement practices also enhances our self-discipline and our physical well-being. When we surround ourselves with soothing colors and inspirational music, we feel nurtured and uplifted. When we do not create a balance among the different aspects of our health, our system rebels. Usually this is first experienced as physical exhaustion but also manifests in emotional instability or depression and mental confusion.

EMOTIONAL, MENTAL, AND SPIRITUAL HEALTH

Neglect of emotional and mental health is neglect of the inner work needed to evolve the soul. The inner strength and stability necessary to solve problems and to stand firm, poised in spirit, are evidence of emotional, mental, and spiritual health. When the inner nature is still, serene, unruffled, quiet, and clear, the intuition delivers accurate impressions from the True Self. Clarity of intuition is difficult, if not impossible, when emotions or the outer environment impinges upon the mind.

Everything we see, hear, touch, and read impacts us, giving

When the inner nature is still, serene, unruffled, quiet, and clear, the intuition delivers accurate impressions from the True Self.

color and movement to our emotions. Unless we are aware, every whim and fancy in the environment may captivate us. Roberto Assagioli emphasizes the profound influence our surroundings have on our psychology, pointing out that we can pollute our psychological environment just as we pollute our physical environment. Aggression, violence, fear, depression and despondency, greed, and harmful competitiveness are some of the external "poisons" that affect our psychological health. To acquire and maintain sound emotional and mental health, Assagioli advises that we eliminate these poisons, both externally and internally.

For example, being in the presence of someone who is endlessly chattering is a form of psychological pollution demanding our energy and potentially drawing us off center. Our goal in maintaining emotional and mental health is to increase our awareness of our inner state. In this way, we stay alert to such situations that can drain our energy and deprive us of our sense of self.

The discipline of regular meditation increases our awareness of our inner state so that we are increasingly able to hold an attitude of meditation throughout the day in our ordinary activities. Stilling the mind allows us to consciously connect to the True Self, enhancing our awareness of a higher plan and honing our intuition and dreams as sources of information and direction. Meditation leads to contemplation, in which we enter into that silence that allows us to tap the Divine Mind. Our goal in meditation is to discover the faculties and powers of the mind, eventually tapping the truth at its source and entering into the mind of God.

From this perspective, our emotional, mental, and spiritual well-being arises from our being in the world but not of it. We do not turn our back upon the world but face it from the level of our soul. We look clear-eyed upon the world of human affairs without falling prey to its illusions. The love of our soul begins to pour

Our goal in meditation is to discover the faculties and powers of the mind, eventually tapping the truth at its source and entering into the mind of God.

through us, and we merge into an awareness of the good of all humanity.

SYNTHESIS

Over and over, we bring the shadow to the light for examination, and gradually we see ourselves as we really are, not as we wish to be, or assume ourselves to be.

Although we may not gaze at it directly, our shadow pervades our life and thus our service. We act from our shadow of service whenever we neglect our well-being as servers and when we react to those we serve with rejection, blame, superiority, guilt, anger, or fear. Our inner desire to be whole urges us to confront our shadow and face our conflicts about giving and receiving service.

Meeting our shadow of service permits us to develop an ongoing and right relationship with it, to expand awareness of self, and to unearth buried potentials and hidden motivations. The shadow is both a container of darkness and a beacon pointing toward the light. With honest self-examination, we gain more complete knowledge of our conscious and unconscious motivations. Standing free of guilt associated with our negative feelings and actions about life and service, we achieve a genuine acceptance of ourselves and those we serve. By recognizing the projections that color our opinion of those we serve, we cease adding our personal darkness to the density of the collective shadow.

Choosing to learn from and with those we serve requires time, commitment, and skill on the continuum of change from outer to inner focus. Over and over, we bring the shadow to the light for examination, and gradually we see ourselves as we really are, not as we wish to be, or assume ourselves to be. This exercise of the willingness to meet the shadow of service builds the first step toward True Service.

PART TWO

The Stages
of Service

To serve—that we may learn,

that we may grow.

$\mathscr{I}$NTRODUCTION

$\mathscr{E}$volution infers a continuum of development rather than discrete categories. The seven stages of evolution of the soul describe the developmental nature of a person's individuation process. As we gain life experiences and actualize our potentialities, we come into our full humanness. We evolve into an authentic self that reflects our wholeness. We become the very best we are capable of being.

The stages also reflect a deepening relationship with the Absolute and how that deepening relationship impacts our motivation to serve others. Because development spirals rather than marches in a line, we can always drop down to a lower stage from wherever we are in the moment. This often happens under stress. Usually, such reversion provides an opportunity for reassessment, recommitment, and new growth. It is possible, however, for an individual to revert and to choose to stay stuck in the old pattern.

By contrast, it is not possible to skip stages of development without negative consequences. To dance freely, one must first master walking, rhythm, and a myriad of other discrete movement and listening skills. Just so, the evolution of the soul through service requires the acquisition and integration of skills *at beginning, intermediate, and advanced levels. The way the soul expresses through the individual is unique to the individual.*

STRUCTURE OF PART TWO

Stages One through Four focus on one's relationship with the outside world:

Stage One: Awakening to Serve
Stage Two: Work Ethic
Stage Three: Missionary Attitude
Stage Four: Wounded Healer

In Stage One, individuals have little or no motivation to help others, focusing primarily on caring for their own physical and material needs. Those in Stage Two look to work to meet their physical and material needs; as doers, helping others is a natural extension of their work ethic. Those in Stages Three and Four serve with the often unconscious motive of having someone or something outside themselves meet their physical and emotional needs.

Stages Five through Seven focus on one's relationship with one's innermost self and with the Absolute:

Stage Five: Healing the Healer
Stage Six: Selfless Action
Stage Seven: Beyond the Physical

In Stages Five and Six, individuals attend to the spiritual well-being of both self and others through selfless service. Stage Five moves into self-responsibility for the inner state. At the highest stage of service, Stage Six, the server has no attachment to the form and outcome of the service. People at this stage may be identified as mystics; they *are* service. In Stage Seven, souls continue to serve after death. Because little is known of Stage Seven, it is described only briefly.

In each stage, primary characteristics are delineated in the margin of the first page. These characteristics serve to orient readers so they can easily see the progression from stage to stage. As one works with the book, these characteristics also provide a quick reference to assist in identifying to which stage one reverts when in crisis. The characteristics are:

- **Statement:** The statement reflects the individual's world view.

- **Salient Fear:** The salient fear reflects the underlying reason why individuals at this stage create obstacles to the soul's full expression. The soul's potential expression is unconditional love; fear creates the obstacles to expression of that love.

- **Core Learning:** The core learning reflects the quality individuals can develop from the blows of their life experiences within each stage. The core learning is the gift to the self.

- **Primary Gift:** Individuals in each stage have a primary gift they offer the world.

- **Transitional Shift:** To move from one stage to the next individuals must surrender one orientation for another. The transitional shifts lead one from a life with an outer focus to a life of inner contemplation at one with action.

In the following chapters, each of the first six stages has four sections defined and delineated as follows.

DESCRIPTION OF THE STAGE

Human development encompasses the physical, emotional, mental, and spiritual aspects and the interaction of any and all of these. The norms for development are ranges rather than absolute markers. For example, most children walk at one year; however, the normal range is from nine to eighteen months. Similarly, although there is an ideal time at which an individual passes through each of the first four Stages of Service, delays occur for one reason or another. The example for each stage was chosen because it is extreme enough to be clear. In reality, each stage holds a whole range of possibilities for its expression.

PROCESS OF THE STAGE

Each stage includes:

- **The State of the Self**, which discusses the way in which the individual defines him- or herself in relationship to the inner and outer struggles of life.

- **World View**, which delineates the relationship of the self with work, others, and life purpose.

- **Relationship with God**, which presents the individual's definition of "God" and the place of religion and spirituality in the person's life.

- **Predominate Shadow Issues**, which identifies issues of projection, denial, and neglect specific to the most salient issues for inner work. This section reflects the content of Chapter Four: The Shadow of Service.

- **Mode of Service**, which discusses the manner and motivation of how the individual serves and is served. Mode of Service, defined in Chapter Three: The Dimensions of Service, includes:

  - duty and the development of the aspects of the will: strong will, good will, skillful will, and Transpersonal Will,

  - charity and attitudes toward giving and receiving,

- purification, and
- devotion.

TRANSITIONING TO THE NEXT STAGE

This section describes the shifts in self-identification, world view, and relationship with God that occur as an individual moves out of one stage of evolution and into the next. Typically, an inner struggle initiates each shift. The struggle manifests itself when disillusionment with the current view of self and others occurs concomitantly with a desire for change. Within each stage, individuals seek to find a better way to be in the world.

SUPPORT FOR THE STAGE

Individuals benefit from support of their concerns and vulnerabilities while capitalizing on their strengths and capabilities. Suggestions in this section address the physical, social, emotional, mental, and spiritual well-being unique to each stage.

STAGE ONE

Awakening to Serve

During the Second World War, my family raised laying hens and marketed eggs. I loved animals and soon selected three hens as pets, naming them Reddy, Specky and Dirty. The three followed me everywhere, allowing me to dress them in doll clothes and push them in my buggy. They often roosted under my bedroom window at night. They were my faithful and loyal friends.

Periodically, my father ordered newborn chicks through the Sears Roebuck & Company catalog. Once an order of a hundred chicks arrived deformed from being incubated and hatched too quickly. I pleaded unsuccessfully with my father not to destroy them. I wanted to do everything I could to help these chicks and didn't see that it mattered that they were all handicapped. I wanted my three hen friends to know of my concern and willingness to help. After all, their loyalty as playmates was helping me through a sometimes scary childhood.

In that moment I knew I had been born to serve. I was certain we, animals as well as people, were on earth to help one another. I was six years old.

DESCRIPTION:
AWAKENING TO SERVE

The Awakening to Serve process develops naturally in a young child. When early nurturance meets our physical and emotional needs, we evolve a healthy awareness of and desire to serve. Early life experiences plant and nurture critical seeds within the psyche that eventually flower as spiritual potential for service.

In my childhood, these critical seeds were numerous and varied. I grew up during the Second World War and learned about the influence people and countries had on one another. Because my family and many others in our small town were of German descent, I became aware of the effects of prejudice. Through my parents and the Lutheran Church I attended, I received an unspoken message emphasizing the prime importance of helping others. The fact that my maternal grandmother was deaf and one of my aunts was brain-injured increased my awareness of those with special needs. In addition, I observed my parents' emphasis on hard work, self-reliance, and responsibility as they raised their family by living off the land and wasting nothing. I incorporated all these values as I formed a sense of my own self.

As a very young child, I had an inherent sense that something was wrong with me. I identified this as something defective with my brain and the way I thought and communicated. This belief planted one of the most important seeds related to my future life and work, that of concern about the health and well-being of the human mind.

As part of the individuation process, I often thought about what my purpose was to be, proclaiming to my parents and myself that I was not going to waste my life. Intuiting that I was here to help others, I questioned how to bring my purpose into reality. From observing my family and the church, I sensed that pleasing

STATEMENT:
Who am I?

CORE LEARNING:
Self-identity

SALIENT FEAR:
If no one tells me who I am, I remain lost.

PRIMARY GIFT:
Emotional sensitivity

TRANSITIONAL SHIFT:
Surrender of self-absorption for purposeful activity

others, negating myself, and working hard were all part of the answer.

Unless children experience being given to in an accepting, loving way, they fail to establish a sense of self, an identity as an individual separate from others. As a result, they do not learn to differentiate their needs from those of others. They experience a loss or sense of separation from love from other people and from the love of God. From my childhood, I brought forward into adolescence and adulthood a tendency to adapt to the needs of others and to negate my own value and voice. As a consequence, I felt unloved and unloving. In my twenties I made a conscious choice to take action to reawaken the experience of love and connection I had lost in my youth. Remembering that animals had kindled my love in my childhood, I acquired a puppy. With this decision, I knew I had taken the first healing step towards rediscovering that I was capable of receiving and giving love.

Depending on the degree of the sense of separation from love, the arrested emotional development may result in a state of egocentricity or narcissism extending into adulthood. Children who do not experience being given to become adults who cannot give or receive. They become stalled in a psychological state of unmet needs. Lacking a sense of self, their psychic energy is available only for seeking ways to have their needs met in the outside world through material goods, pleasure, relationships, or substances. They feel they have nothing to give to others, and they suspect that giving to others necessitates having less for themselves. Because they feel empty and disconnected from others and from God, the thought of giving something away is frightening and unimaginable. Such individuals experience great suffering until they are able to address the primal cause of their pain.

Out of their own experience of intense physical and emotional pain emerges the gift that Stage One individuals extend, often

Unless children experience being given to in an accepting, loving way, they fail to establish a sense of self, an identity as an individual separate from others.

unwittingly: their emotional sensitivity to the distress of others. Although self-preoccupied, they often express a strong desire to have deep bonds with family and friends and are willing to work toward that end. Their pain also creates an openness to receiving help through counseling or therapy and to broadening their world view by exploring alternative philosophies. Their sensitivity and openness, however, reflect Stage One's undifferentiated boundaries between self and others. They tend to see their own pain reflected in the pain of others. Through this empathic experience, they meet their emotional need for connection and validate their own suffering.

To move out of Stage One, these individuals must become aware that life is about more than meeting one's own needs. They must examine the cause of their suffering in order to move away from it. To examine the cause of suffering is to awaken regarding self and service to others.

I once spoke to a church group about service as a path of the heart and as a way to live life with purpose and enthusiasm. As part of my talk, I distributed a questionnaire and asked the participants to rate themselves on their attitudes concerning helping others. The ratings ranged from one, representing being unwilling to serve, to five, representing willing service.

As the group became engrossed in the questionnaire, a young man sitting in the front row caught my attention. He appeared to be in agony, grimacing, staring into space, and then either circling ones or skipping items. I had not anticipated that someone in the audience would find the exercise painful or be unable to examine how he or she viewed serving.

After my speech, I sought out and met Randy and asked how he felt about the questionnaire. He responded that he was in so much emotional pain in his life that he could not and would not

Their sensitivity and openness, however, reflect Stage One's undifferentiated boundaries between self and others. They tend to see their own pain reflected in the pain of others.

help another person. He added that he never thought about helping others. I asked if we could stay in touch and Randy agreed.

Over the five years in which I have observed Randy, he has exemplified the distortion that occurs when one stays stuck in the earliest stage of awareness of service. Focusing primarily on his own physical and emotional needs, he has been essentially unable to direct his energies towards consciously assisting another.

Establishing one's personal physical and emotional space and one's beliefs and attitudes are essential steps to developing a sense of self.

PROCESS OF AWAKENING TO SERVE

STATE OF THE SELF

The task that faces someone in the first stage of awareness to serve is the development of a personality, a sense of self-identity. Key questions for these individuals are "Who am I?" and "How are my values and beliefs the same and different from those of others?" Establishing one's personal physical and emotional space and one's beliefs and attitudes are essential steps to developing a sense of self. To accomplish this, one must address emotional wounds that have resulted in the abdication of personal power and in seeking validation outside oneself.

Unable to discern that his identity is separate from that of others, Randy is nearly devoid of a sense of self. He is unaware of what he, as an individual, feels, believes, and values; therefore, he has little confidence or trust in the validity of his own experience. He seeks validation of his personal value, decisions, and actions from others. He fails to remember and integrate what he has learned from his life experiences. Because he continually looks outside himself for his physical and psychological safety, he often is not aware of the physical sensation of being in his body.

Randy repeatedly finds himself in abusive and co-dependent relationships because he fails to trust himself to accurately discern the intentions of others. This misreading of people and situations often appears as confusion, indecision, and a lack of "common sense." He is unable to separate his own emotional space from that of another and believes others hold the key to his well-being. He is forever seeking and never finding. Fearing that his physical and psychological needs will never be met, he exhibits narcissistic tendencies and is totally self-absorbed. Rarely is he able to identify his projections and take responsibility for his perceptions and choices.

WORLD VIEW

Individuals in Stage One believe the outside world holds the potential for their salvation. They keep searching in relationships, addictive substances, material goods, or work situations for the someone or something outside themselves that will meet their physical and psychological needs. They feel victimized, disempowered, and frustrated by a world they perceive as thwarting their attempts to have healthy personal or work relationships.

Lacking self-identity, those in this stage are unsure of their purpose and mission in life. In reality, their purpose centers on developing a sense of self.

Lacking self-identity, those in this stage are unsure of their purpose and mission in life. In reality, their purpose centers on developing a sense of self. Once they experience a successful relationship or work situation, they begin to shift their world view. The knowledge that they are participating in and contributing to the world strengthens them. They begin to make changes in their attitude and behavior and move away from feeling victimized by circumstances.

RELATIONSHIP WITH GOD

Persons in this stage may pray or reflect on their lives, but they do so in a hurried fashion or for short periods, returning always to their outer preoccupation. They fail to use the consistent self-effort needed to develop a spiritual life. Because they sense, but do not fully experience, the fullness of the beauty of their inner divinity, they taste, but do not persist in, regular spiritual practice. In her book, *The Interior Castle*, St. Teresa of Avila, the sixteenth century Spanish mystic, compares a person in this stage to a bee who busies itself in gathering nectar, but periodically manages to fly simply "to ponder the grandeur and majesty of its God."

What is unique for Stage One individuals, however, is that their openness coexists with an inability to integrate spiritual principles into their personalities and to practice them in a meaningful way.

Prayers of those in Stage One often reflect a desire to control or use God to meet their needs. Prayers tend to be supplications, such as "Do this for me" or "Give me what I want." Those in this stage also tend to bargain with God by saying, "If you do this, I will do that." Prayers are rarely used to express gratitude or devotion.

A Stage One person may express their openness by seeking to learn self-help techniques, psychological approaches, or spiritual teachings. Randy's attendance at my presentation expressed this openness. What is unique for Stage One individuals, however, is that their openness coexists with an inability to integrate spiritual principles into their personalities and to practice them in a mean-ingful way. Such people have a tremendous gap between psycho-logical and spiritual knowledge and the application of that knowl-edge in their lives. This discrepancy significantly increases the level of inner conflict, anxiety, uncertainty, and frustration. The lack of conscious awareness of the True Self and inattention to the discov-ery of meaning and purpose in life compounds this discrepancy.

PREDOMINANT SHADOW ISSUES

In this stage a struggle exists between the outer and inner realities. The outer persists in its strength and position and con-tinually wins attention over the inner. When the pull to the outer world is strong, those in this stage are indecisive. They may vacillate on questions of even minor importance. Others in this stage may find decision-making in certain matters easier than in others. For example, they may be clear about deciding where they want to live and what job to take yet be fearful and anxious about how to have healthy relationships with friends and family.

PROJECTION

Because those who are awakening to serve preoccupy themselves with their own survival, they tend to identify with the suffering of others. They project onto others their own sense of helplessness and victimization. They have difficulty separating their own suffering from that of others. They are liable to project their fear of rejection and abandonment by assuming responsibility for another's feelings and experiences. The inner reality of those in this stage is one of sentiment, which results in emotions coloring both thought and behavior.

Out of a sense of powerlessness, those in this stage tend to use passive resistance as an attempt to acquire personal power. Passive resistance is a way to control the emotions and decisions of others in order to meet one's own needs. For example, out of a need to please one might agree to do something but not follow through with the action. People feel victimized and betrayed by passive resistant behavior and often respond by withdrawing. In turn, this withdrawal results in the passive person feeling rejected and victimized. Passive resistance arises from an individual's constant need to prove her power by asking others to take responsibility for her. In the process, the individual gives her power away.

Pride in this stage conceals or disguises itself as specialness. An individual expresses an exaggerated opinion of himself when there is no evidence to validate this. One can be prideful about one's failures, being "successful" in achieving the least or in having the

Out of a sense of powerlessness, those in this stage tend to use passive resistance as an attempt to acquire personal power. Passive resistance is a way to control the emotions and decisions of others in order to meet one's own needs.

fewest healthy relationships. Pride of failure reflects an arrogant poor-me attitude. Such a person may also be vain, expressing an excessive desire to be admired by others for either positive or negative achievements or appearance.

Those in this stage are vulnerable to becoming attached to those who serve them because they look to others for validation and advice. This tendency makes them susceptible to cults or rigid religions that promise them protection and well-being. For the same reasons, they are vulnerable to substance abuse and other addictions and to attachments to relationships and material goods. Their emotional neediness has the potential of draining the energies of those who help them.

DENIAL

Those in this stage are often unaware of their hidden potential and subsequently deny their inner resources. To them, success and achievement in the world seem beyond their reach. Because they do not feel connected to their potential, they become preoccupied with their limitations and lack, conveying a pessimism about their value as a person.

Evasion of service in this stage takes the form of preoccupation with self, reflecting an understandable need to focus energies on personal survival. For example, occasionally Randy moves out of his state of emotional and spiritual darkness and considers working more diligently on his emotional healing. He says he is ready to accept help for his physical and emotional well-being and often verbalizes a yearning for a spiritual connection to God. He repeatedly takes steps forward and then retreats again into his state of insecurity and preoccupation with the world. He says he wants to be responsible for his life yet hesitates to take the first steps toward self-responsibility.

Those in this stage are vulnerable to becoming attached to those who serve them because they look to others for validation and advice.

Randy's attraction to work situations that are beyond his marketable skills, level of competence, and work experience illustrates his incompetence. Likewise, he desires meaningful personal relationships but is unprepared to be an adult partner. He fantasizes that his inner conflict will stop the day that he "makes it big" personally and professionally.

Randy focuses on physical survival. He searches for his identity through pleasure, possessions, and business affairs. He expects external circumstances or other people to eventually succeed in fulfilling his physical, emotional, and spiritual needs. He has difficulty learning how to live in the world in a practical way to meet daily needs. He wants the world to take care of him.

Because Randy believes his inner stability is dependent on the external world, he feels compelled to attempt to control outer circumstances. Lonely and dependent on the emotional validation of others, he often seeks advice but rarely chooses to follow it. In this way, he maintains his belief system and has some control in his uncontrollable life. He also attempts to gain control of his inner life through obsessive or compulsive thinking and behavior.

Evasion of service in this stage takes the form of preoccupation with self, reflecting an understandable need to focus energies on personal survival.

NEGLECT

Some adults stuck in Stage One may be so self-absorbed as to be identified as mentally ill. If assisted by a routine, boundaries, and structure, they can usually function in the world fairly well. The struggle between inner and outer realities produces much anxiety and desperation for someone like Randy. Attached to the outer for validation and not ready to trust his inner self, Randy persists in his self-preoccupation. Because of his strong need for validation and confirmation from the outer world, he repeatedly reaches out for help but does not know how to receive and accept it. Consequently, he experiences intense aloneness and remains insecure.

Randy often expresses an emotional detachment from the world and from an identification with humanity. He feels alone and different and unable to function independently in the world. The world, to him, *is* him. Yet, he yearns to experience a true connection with himself and others.

MODE OF SERVICE

Because the dominant struggle in this stage concerns learning self-identity and self-responsibility, the mode of service focuses primarily on **duty**. Although sensitive and sympathetic to the pain of others, the individual is not yet ready to engage in charity, conscious purification, or to have a true devotional life.

In this stage, the person's primary duty is to himself. This duty is one of establishing healthy boundaries in personal, social, and work relationships and of developing a strong and skillful will.

In this stage, the person's primary duty is to himself. This duty is one of establishing healthy boundaries in personal, social, and work relationships and of developing a strong and skillful will. These are the major goals as those in this stage move away from inertia and absence of initiative. In becoming self-responsible, they need to develop the will's qualities of initiation and persistence. At times they take the initiative to participate in some activity but are unable to follow through with their intention. This makes acquiring practical skills and completing tasks a priority. It is common for those in this stage to compensate for their lack of skills by overusing the **strong will**. When this occurs, they impose their will on other people in an attempt to meet their own needs.

Giving does not come easily for those in this stage. Because they devote their energy to survival issues, they have little to use for other endeavors. Although they feel as though they "should" give to others, giving feels like a sacrifice. This feeling is voiced as "If I give to you, I won't have enough for myself." Their attitude tends to be one of giving to get. Yet at times, they express a desire to learn and grow and have glimpses of what it might be like to feel more connected with other people.

Those in the initial awareness stage of service identify with suffering and represent the first path of Buddhism called the "suffering of suffering." Being self-preoccupied, either they cannot detach from their own pain long enough to serve others or they lose the psychological boundary between their needs and the needs of others.

Nevertheless, those in this stage are often kind and enjoy helping others with immediate physical needs. They want to reach out to others but cannot sustain their helping because they lack sufficient energy or skillful will. Often they view responsibilities in life as obligations and have difficulty following through on their intentions.

Randy, like many in this stage, is sensitive to the pain of others. He makes periodic forays into doing good works and does concrete and short-term helping, such as a onetime raking of leaves for a neighbor. Helping that gives him immediate feedback makes him feel good about his "sacrifice." Because he has difficulty focusing on productivity and self-responsibility, Randy does not do well in a work setting. Like many in this stage, he is not consistently financially independent.

It is common for many in this stage to have a strong desire to experience a relationship with God. They may go to church or belong to a structured group in an attempt to bring meaning and order to life and also to have contact with people. Depending on the level of development of the strong and skillful will, however, their motivation is not at the level of seeing devotion as duty. In fact, their attendance is likely to be sporadic, and they will frequently be late.

It is common for many in this stage to have a strong desire to experience a relationship with God.

TRANSITIONING TO STAGE TWO: THE WORK ETHIC

What may appear to be a small step for the personality is a major step of the soul; the first call of spiritual unfoldment has been heard.

For a person to move out of Stage One, two insights are crucial: that the struggle is with the self *and* that life is more than meeting one's own needs. These transformative insights are rudimentary, barely dawning, like a child's first attempts to stand and walk. Yet they are strong enough to support the important and seemingly unusual commitment of stepping at least briefly into the inner world of spiritual essence. At some level they know they will be able to sustain this connection for longer periods of time. St. Teresa comments that people at this stage have done quite a bit simply by entering the castle of the soul, even through they cannot see its beauty. This step inward opens the way for a healthy ego to develop.

What may appear to be a small step for the personality is a major step of the soul; the first call of spiritual unfoldment has been heard. Such people have a brief glimpse of the awareness of the suffering of others. They do not yet see that the suffering of others relates in any real way to that of their own. Preoccupation with self still exists and their own suffering and search in the outer world remain the center of their life. Yet the glimpse of others' suffering plants the seed of "otherness"; companion souls exist who are on a similar venture. It is time to prepare to receive this first hint of Truth.

At the same time, they awaken to the awareness that to live is to be productive, to make things happen, to transform chaos into order, to fulfill one's duty by becoming financially independent. Society has needs; family has needs. The individual has a duty to help make the world "work."

As the person focuses more and more attention and energy on earning a living and achieving success in the outside world, transition from Stage One to Stage Two begins. Stage Two is more demanding than Stage One in its practicality and level of responsibility to others. Feeling personally called to have an inner life and responding to this call by cultivating a "work ethic" in the home or in the work world marks one's placement in Stage Two.

SUPPORT FOR STAGE ONE

There are many ways to support oneself and to be supported by others while in Stage One and while bridging from Stage One to Stage Two. This support involves:

- preparation for work through education, training and experience;

- exploration of how one's desires might be fulfilled and expressed in the world;

- recognition of a need for a steadier commitment to prayer; and

- awareness of obligations or duty to family, community, and the world.

Because of the lack of integration and pervasive emotional needs, one in this stage may not recognize the help and support extended. Support, therefore, needs to be specific and practical and its value periodically reviewed.

Persons in Stage One benefit greatly from compassionate emotional support while they learn practical skills such as short-term goal setting. Most helpful is a step-by-step approach to living a healthy and responsible physical, social, and emotional life. They also need direct and immediate feedback regarding the consequences of their actions and the effectiveness of their efforts at self-awareness. Feedback is most effective when given concomitantly with exercises for strengthening and developing the will.

Persons in Stage One benefit greatly from compassionate emotional support while they learn practical skills such as short-term goal setting.

Individuals in this stage play a unique and vital role for servers in later stages who receive valuable spiritual lessons about service by knowing and serving those in Stage One.

Cognitive or behaviorally based psychotherapeutic approaches are appropriate. With such support they can learn from the consequences of looking outside themselves for validation and develop a greater sense of self. Hands-on healing or gentle body work also supports the physical and emotional well-being of those in this stage.

Individuals in this stage play a unique and vital role for servers in later stages who receive valuable spiritual lessons about service by knowing and serving those in Stage One. Dr. Mikao Usui, discoverer of Reiki, an ancient form of healing, told of his learning from Stage One individuals.

Dr. Usui took Reiki into the largest slum of Kyoto. Disguised as a beggar, he worked from sunup until sundown for seven years, healing those in the beggar camp of their physical illnesses of tuberculosis, impetigo, leprosy, and emphysema. Once they were healed, he sent some of the young men to a Zen temple to receive a new name, a job, and a life as an honorable citizen.

One day as he walked around the compound, he saw the familiar faces of these same young men. Their reason for returning to the slum startled him. They had worked at the temple but were only allowed to stay two years. Then the monks sent them out to compete in the life of the city. This life was difficult, so they decided that being beggars required less work and fewer responsibilities.

Dr. Usui was heartbroken and he realized that he had only thought about physical healing and had not taught the beggars about honest daily work, respect and gratitude. He applied this learning wisely. From that time he served only those people who needed help and who were spiritually ready to receive the gifts of Reiki. He also formulated the five principles of Reiki:

- Just for today do not anger.

- Just for today do not worry.

- Count your blessings and show gratitude.

- Do an honest day's job, earn an honest living.

- Be kind to anything that has life.

From that time, he served only those people who needed help and who were spiritually ready to receive the gifts of Reiki.

Stage Two

The Work Ethic

My parents had barely driven away on their vacation, leaving my siblings and me at home with our grandmother, when I ran to the back porch and readied a bucket of strong soap and water. Believing my parents could not afford to paint the outside of our house and being embarrassed because it needed painting, I had long awaited the opportunity that now presented itself. I would scrub the entire exterior of our house by hand while my parents were out of town. After all, I had already hand-scrubbed the back porch.

A few days later, I overheard my grandmother tell her friends that I was a good child because I worked very hard. I concluded that people like hard workers because they do more than their share of work in the world.

I remember consciously deciding to be responsible and do my part in the world. I was twelve years old.

DESCRIPTION:
THE WORK ETHIC

As individuals move into Stage Two, work, with its intensity and financial benefits, is what gives meaning to life. Whereas in Stage One the person conducts an unfocused search for identity, by Stage Two, work and productivity have become the focus. Individuals feel that if they just work hard and well enough and make enough money, everything will be all right. The goal is to lead a productive life by fulfilling one's duty to earn a living. Work has its own benefits and only coincidentally is it a service.

In Stage Two, the individual understands the relationship between a goal and the procedure and skills needed to reach it and uses this knowledge as the basis of action. Through work, an individual supports self and family, transforms chaos into order, and generally fulfills obligations and responsibilities. These achievements validate one's importance to the world. Experiencing the tangible fruits of one's labors is uplifting and exhilarating, especially when rewarded by the esteem of others. Such feedback builds self-esteem and perpetuates the work ethic.

When children do not understand the relationship between their goals or desires and their ability to create a system for meeting them, they become discouraged and refuse to continue practicing the task. A child begins what may be a lifelong pattern of procrastination, lack of initiative, disorganization, and an inability to carry out a goal to its successful completion. These patterns eventually become obstacles to the fulfillment of their potential in life.

The opposite pattern may emerge in children who have felt emotionally rejected. They often clearly see that how they do what they do brings specific results and learn to control or manipulate people to get what they want. In this way, they meet

STATEMENT:
All my problems will be solved through action in the world.

CORE LEARNING:
Use of power

SALIENT FEAR:
If I don't control the world, it will control me.

PRIMARY GIFT:
Productivity

TRANSITIONAL SHIFT:
Surrender of meeting individual material needs for doing good in the world

their emotional needs for acceptance and inclusion.

Those in Stage Two have many gifts because they are the do-ers and wage earners of the world. Those who work for work's sake serve as the "salt of the earth," the mainstay of society. They often have a wide range of interests and play a major role in mak-ing things happen in the arena of family, church, career, educa-tion, politics, economics, technology, culture, and community. They can be generous in their contributions to charity and good works. Because their will is both strong and skillful, they are com-petent and productive. Whether engaged in skilled or unskilled labor, mastering their work and being financially secure are im-portant to them. Someone can be in the work ethic stage in any kind of work; leaders in education, social, economic, and political arenas are often in Stage Two.

I first met Russ when, in the face of a virulent form of brain cancer, he asked for my support. Pale and thin, the once-robust Russ looked up at me from his hospital bed and asked, "What do I do now? Why can't I turn this deadly cancer around if I say I am changing the way I think and the way I live my life? I have changed my attitude. Why hasn't my changed attitude changed my cancer?"

By the age of thirty-six, Russ had lived a life of power and achievement. He relished his association with national political leaders and his friendships with the rich and famous. He enjoyed all the indulgences of physical and material wealth. In childhood he had experienced tremendous psychological trauma when he witnessed his younger brother's death by drowning. He felt emo-tionally alone and excluded as his parents withdrew into their own grief. Through a chance experience as a teenager, he discovered that he could manipulate groups of people to do what he wanted.

"All I had to do," he said, "was become an activist and my classmates would follow my lead. Then, in college, when I read

Whereas in Stage One the person conducts an unfocused search for identity, by Stage Two, work and productivity have become the focus.

Machiavelli's *The Prince*, I knew I could get people to do anything I wanted if I just followed the directions in this book. It was then I decided that I wanted to become the most powerful person in the world." By his admission he had successfully used this method of leadership to manipulate an entire nation into voting for his party's candidate as the next president. He believed that the ultimate position of power belonged, not to the elected leader, but to the person responsible for the leader's election.

Those who work for work's sake serve as the "salt of the earth," the mainstay of society.

On an inner level, Russ knew he was to stop his manipulation of power in mid-life and retire to an academic setting. He looked forward to the day he could share the wisdom of what he had learned with the next generation. He repeatedly delayed making this life change until after the next election, and the next, and the next. The cancer finally made the choice for him.

Russ was in the second stage of awareness of service. Through the work ethic he had learned tremendous organizational and leadership skills. In the process, he became seduced by success and satisfied his need for self-validation through wealth, power, and pleasure. To assure himself of his own power, he became adept at manipulating others. Yet he had glimpses of another way to be. He had always heard the voice of his inner self calling him to serve from a place of greater awareness. Even when his illness began, he knew a spiritual test faced him.

PROCESS OF THE WORK ETHIC

STATE OF THE SELF

Whereas the Stage One individual searches unsuccessfully for a sense of self in a variety of ways, Stage Two settles on work and productivity as the source of personal worth. Participation in social, cultural, and economic ventures is a priority; they tend to avoid exploring the depths of the self. During this stage, life is not used as a classroom for psychological and spiritual growth.

WORLD VIEW

Through the discipline of work, individuals establish a sense of control over their lives.

Those in Stage Two view work as the primary way to bring order to life and find security in an unstable world. Through the discipline of work, individuals establish a sense of control over their lives. Whether engaged in skilled or unskilled labor, they value earning a living that supports themselves and their families. They search in the world for their peace and happiness, looking to other people and outer events as the source of feedback that they are worthwhile.

As active and productive participants in society, they view the world as a place to be mastered. Competition is an essential part of gaining this mastery. Whether a householder, parent, laborer, or professional, they strive to improve their skills and competence. They may feel a strong sense of responsibility to family members and to their community. Their prevailing attitude toward the world is to work well, work hard, and look for praise and rewards in what one does in one's life.

RELATIONSHIP WITH GOD

During this stage, individuals begin to hear a call to move deeper into the interior of themselves. Knowing that effort and discipline will be necessary to maintain this inner awareness while working in the world, they hesitate to respond. Using St. Teresa's analogy of the castle as the soul, individuals in this stage move closer to the center of the castle. They now begin to feel an attraction from the center. They perceive this either as a personal call from God or as a call from and for good. God invites them to respond personally. The call comes through religious or social action organizations, books, people, and events in one's life. St. Teresa writes that "hearing His voice is a greater trial than not hearing it."

PREDOMINANT SHADOW ISSUES

Stage Two individuals seek to solve their struggle concerning the pull between their inner and outer world by ignoring their inner life and increasing their efforts to find security in the outer world. Stage Two focuses on action in the world and its rewards. These rewards may be the ability to materially support relationships, consumerism, recreation, or in academic or professional success. Eventually, the individual notices that the rewards neither last nor satisfy an inner hunger.

The conflict between the inner and outer worlds of those in Stage Two evidences in their inability to engage in the inner work needed to address their hidden motivations. Because they fear looking within, numerous shadow issues pervade their work, careers, businesses, and personal relationships.

PROJECTION

Work Ethic individuals experience some level of success in the world and have a sense of control and power over their outer lives. As a result, they often project their need for control onto others. This projection exemplifies their hidden and unexamined fears about losing control and security and may materialize as contempt for weakness and hunger for physical or material pleasures. Projections in the Work Ethic stage take the form of power and fame, pride, sentiment, and attachment.

The conflict between the inner and outer worlds of those in Stage Two evidences in their inability to engage in the inner work needed to address their hidden motivations.

Regardless of their personas, Stage Two individuals typically project the shadow by blaming others for their inner conflicts.

Characteristic of the shadow's projection is categorical or right/wrong, black/white, either/or, we/they thinking. This characteristic leads to strong feelings of competitiveness and victimization. A desire for inner power feeds pride and is the motivation for being competitive, for acquiring outer authority, and for wanting rewards and recognition. Lacking an inner sense of worth and validation, persons can use work as a way to obtain a position of authority and satisfy their desire for power and fame. Their desire for outer power actually reflects an inner belief in powerlessness. There are many instances of moral, upstanding business people caught in shady deals, embezzling money, cheating on taxes, or using authority to engage in sexual misconduct.

Out of fear of losing power, persons in Stage Two often face painful conflicts of values. To retain their power, they may violate principles, dominate others, disregard employees' personal needs, tell white lies, or sell out in other small ways. The pressure of high-tension environments can lead to ego inflation with failure becoming shameful. They may overdevelop certain skills. They also may cultivate extroverted ambitious personalities like some sales representatives, athletes, politicians, or entrepreneurs. They may forget how to thrive outside the limelight or how to receive riches from solitude and from within themselves. By contrast, Stage Two people with more private *personas* such as artists and writers may keep their ambition and greed hidden in the shadow. Regardless of their *personas*, Stage Two individuals typically project the shadow by blaming others for their inner conflicts. This results in divisiveness and loss of emotional safety in families and in the workplace.

Those in this stage can overvalue achievement to such an extent that they sacrifice other aspects of their lives and become workaholics, pouring their lifeblood into a venture. The workplace may contribute to these vulnerabilities by setting up untenable work loads, unrealistic sales quotas, and social, martini lunches. The toll this life-style takes manifests in the suffering of loved ones who experience an absent spouse or parent and in the eventual physical and emotional deterioration of the individual.

Regrettably, people can become addicted to work for its emotional rewards. They work harder, achieve more, gain positive feedback, and work even harder. This cycle leads to attachment and pride as they begin to believe themselves and their work to be superior. They become addicted to the "high" of work as it fulfills their need for validation and emotional and spiritual connectedness. They are also prone to addiction to substances, gambling, sex, exercise, or overeating, again searching for spiritual fulfillment outside themselves in the physical and material world.

Because of their chameleon-like adaptability, Stage Two individuals either hide or deny their incompetence.

DENIAL

Those in the Work Ethic stage tend to deny their individuality by adapting themselves to fit into a collective *persona* of a workplace or kind of work. They willingly bury qualities that do not meet the image of their company or the nature of their work. In his book, *Modern Madness*, Douglas LaBier calls such individuals the "working wounded." He describes them as "healthy people adjusted at great emotional cost due to conditions that are good for the advancement of career but not of spirit."

Organizations that demand such conformity exhibit low tolerance for feedback or conflict, support of policies that have disastrous ecological consequences, and dishonesty with customers. Because of their chameleon-like adaptability, Stage Two individuals either hide or deny their incompetence. This can lead to perfectionism and over-preparedness. A person in the Work Ethic stage may pursue advanced degrees or innumerable training courses in the attempt to find the competence they feel they lack.

NEGLECT

For the sake of productivity, achievement, pride, and fame, those in this stage often severely neglect and abuse their physical, emotional, and spiritual well-being. They may abuse the body through the enormous stress that comes from overwork, poor dietary habits, and lack of proper rest and exercise. Health problems develop, such as cardiovascular and other stress-related diseases. Some attend to their physical health but avoid caring for their emotional and spiritual well-being. They fail to learn about their own psychology and to heal and maintain mental health. They also neglect developing a spiritual discipline.

Practicing delayed gratification can be difficult for those in this stage. Impatient to achieve and be productive, they come to expect "fast food service" in all aspects of their life, including physical, emotional, and spiritual changes. The discipline of delayed gratification is preliminary to developing the spiritual quality of detachment.

As the inner life of those in this stage demands attention, the intensity of the struggle between outer and inner realities increases. Even while experiencing much inner conflict, persons persist in their attempts to answer this call through work and their intellect, memory, and will. St. Teresa writes, "Can there be an evil greater than that of being ill at ease in our own house? What hope can we have of finding rest outside of ourselves if we cannot be at rest within?"

MODE OF SERVICE

Those in Stage Two develop a strong sense of **duty** related to service and a beginning interest in charity. Once they have developed a strong, capable, and skillful will, they have the potential to make significant contributions to society. Because of their focus on work for work's sake, those in this stage can lose sight of the relationship of their work to the greater good. They may not be consistent in incorporating the aspect of the good will in their work.

Whereas in Stage One, the individual focused on establishing a **strong will**, in Stage Two, he or she develops the **skillful will**. A strong and skillful will is essential if one is to work competently and productively in the world. They might, however, neglect the good will. A person in this stage can give to others out of a sense of obligation and social duty and not necessarily with an attitude of good will. As their interest is in appearances, achievement, power, and fame, a deep understanding of the broader good of humanity is rarely their motivation for giving.

The motivation to give is at the early steps of Maimonides' levels of giving. As such, they tend to give grudgingly or cheerfully, but less than they could. They may provide appropriately but only after being asked, or they may give significantly before being asked if others know about the gift. They tend not to continue their giving if they do not feel personally appreciated or acknowledged.

Service to others can occur as a by-product of Stage Two's work in the world, not as a purposeful intention out of concern for the whole of humanity. For example, a person in this stage might serve in order to enhance their work resumes. They might see service as an intellectual pursuit or as an opportunity to develop technologies or material goods for financial gain. In general, they consider service coincidental to the form of the work.

Stage Two individuals value others' opinions of them and want others to view them as doing good and being giving. They readily

Because of their focus on work for work's sake, those in this stage can lose sight of the relationship of their work to the greater good.

accept financial obligations to **charity** and to participating in the care and development of their community. They serve with clear action and often with little sentimentality. Because they are self-oriented and see a we/they world, they do not fully grasp the suffering of humanity as a whole. They tend to morally judge others rather than look more deeply into the cause of the suffering that resides beyond behavior. The attitude of someone in this stage might be, "We are all fellow human beings, so let's get on with it."

Those in the work world provide a tremendous valuable and skillful service. They play a major role in making things happen in daily life. Manual laborers, technicians, intellectuals, homemakers, and professionals who focus on their chosen tasks as a way of making their mark on the world provide the foundation of every society. Their efforts ensure our artistic, social, and cultural heritage.

By engaging in family, school, and work tasks, one acquires important practical skills. Individuals develop an attitude of willingness and cooperation as they carry out these tasks. They have a sense of duty to make the world "work" and they prepare themselves to do so through education, training, and experience. The skillful aspect of their will develops and strengthens as they organize and carry out daily activities with concentration, persistence, and deliberation.

When Russ faced his brain cancer, he was unable to mobilize his inner resources to heal himself because he had not developed the use of his will to bring about the outer manifestation of inner change. Even if he had recovered, he might not have been able to shift his energies from an outer preoccupation to an inner journey. It is usually impossible to suddenly shift one's energies from the outer world to the inner world when for years one has focused intently and exclusively on the outer. We cannot suddenly lift a

They have a sense of duty to make the world "work" and they prepare themselves to do so through education, training, and experience.

hundred pound weight without previously having practiced and strengthened our muscles by having first lifted weights of five pounds, then fifteen pounds, then thirty pounds, and so forth. We cannot expect an underdeveloped will to perform tasks it has not been practicing all along.

People in this stage practice giving as a spiritual discipline with an element of fear, and even superstition, of what will happen if they do not give. They can give to maintain appearances of doing good in their lives and in the world. Although they have inner glimpses of a deeper motivation for giving, they depend on outside influences to direct their giving. They step in and out of an inner awareness of a spiritual reality yet continue to look outside for the source of their peace and happiness.

As those in this stage become less self-focused, they sense there is a purpose to life that goes beyond work performance. They have glimmers that a possible meaning of life is available in serving others through serving humanity and God.

Although they have inner glimpses of a deeper motivation for giving, they depend on outside influences to direct their giving.

TRANSITIONING TO STAGE THREE: THE MISSIONARY ATTITUDE

The transition to Stage Three commences when individuals begin to doubt the value of devoting all their time and energy to working in the world and to leisure. Eventually, they can no longer deny the existence of an inner call nor avoid using the strength and skills of their will for the good of themselves and of humanity. Having tried everything imaginable to find peace and happiness in the world, they begin to realize that they have reached the limits of what the outer world has to offer in validating their existence. Although unclear about how they are to be or what they are to do, they know that they need to focus on their realization that some well-defined, recognizable way of impacting change in the world must surely hold the answer. They then begin to accept the validity and steadfastness of an inner calling. They feel an impetus to examine and refocus their psychological and spiritual values and struggle to mobilize their will to bring about this change. The strength of the attachment to the material world, however, often delays the change. For some, like Russ, a threat to security or to life itself is necessary to bring the urgency to change to full conscious awareness.

For the true self to come forward, the personality must move off center stage.

When the individual considers turning inward, he or she experiences deep conflict because the *persona* or personality has firmly established itself as the center of the "universe." This struggle is intense because, as Carl Jung warned, neither the wrong solution nor the right one is easy. Awareness of a deeper self, the true center of the psyche, remains hidden. In normal development, individuals work hard to gain an identity in the world and develop specific attitudes and functions. As awareness deepens, individuals question their *personas*. For the true self to come forward, the personality must move off center stage. Jung writes that "the experience of the self is always a defeat for the ego."

The primary way that those transitioning from Stage Two to Stage Three move their personalities off center stage is to shift their attention away from themselves onto others. The pendulum swings from extreme self-absorption to extreme other-preoccupation as if compensating for the period of overindulgence in materialism and achievement. Just as they once committed to work, they now commit to others in the form of social and religious causes.

SUPPORT FOR STAGE TWO

As in Stage One, the Work Ethic stage is one in which persons look without rather than within for wisdom, insight, and well-being. As such, two major kinds of support are helpful for those in this stage. First, they need assistance in developing capabilities and strengths necessary to master living in the world. Second, they need support to avoid being seduced by the world or lost in material goods or addictions.

Because they are people of action, those in the Work Ethic stage welcome opportunities to acquire, practice, and use their intelligence, will, and talents. They value education, training, and experience. During the Work Ethic stage, it is possible to overdevelop the strong and skillful aspects of the will. It is helpful to focus on using the will for the good of self and others.

Balance and integration are major concerns for those in this stage. Just as they may fail to integrate the will's goodness with its strength and skill, they may compartmentalize aspects of their life. This imbalance manifests in their tendency to sacrifice a personal and family life for a work life. Often they experience a discrepancy between their wisdom and the application of this wisdom. Because of these imbalances, they need support in monitoring the balance between work life, family life, and time in nature.

Periodic reviews of the quality of their physical, mental, emotional, and spiritual life assist in maintaining balance. Often focused on themselves, they may benefit from broadening their world view to include knowledge and acquaintances representing all walks of life.

Those in this stage may ignore the impact of their behavior and work on others. As such, they need support in understanding the effect of their decisions on the well-being of themselves and others, particularly family, friend, and work relationships. This entails a shift of attitude about service and asks that they bridge to recognizing a more meaningful way to serve humanity.

During crises and for problem-solving, individuals in Stage

During the Work Ethic stage, it is possible to overdevelop the strong and skillful aspects of the will.

Two benefit from practical cognitive psychotherapy. They can receive support from self-help books that address physical and emotional health and interpersonal relationships. Because addictions of all forms are a major concern in this stage, participation in twelve-step programs can be particularly helpful.

Spiritually, increased time in prayer supports those in this stage. They may be ready to explore spiritual or religious traditions and to consider serving others as serving God.

Periodic reviews of the quality of their physical, mental, emotional, and spiritual life assist in maintaining balance.

STAGE THREE

The Missionary Attitude

When I was confirmed in the Lutheran church at age thirteen, I vowed to faithfully follow the ten commandments and abide by all of the do's and don'ts of Lutheran theology. One of the "don'ts" was that we were never to think of ourselves and our needs. Another was that we would not use the pronoun "I." One of the "do's" was to sacrifice ourselves for others through some sort of missionary work.

Soon after my confirmation I had two experiences that resulted in my wanting to become a missionary. One afternoon, I heard my deaf grandmother and her mentally handicapped daughter scream as they walked near our home. I discovered to my horror that some children were throwing stones at them. I decided I must help the "less fortunate."

The second significant experience happened soon after when one of the high school students in my small class of eighteen committed suicide. Ruby and I, with most of our classmates, had been in the same class since first grade. For years she had asked for acceptance. Many rejected her because of what she wore, how she smelled, and where she lived. After Ruby's death, I made a promise to sacrifice myself and my own needs to save others from their misery. I was sixteen years old.

DESCRIPTION: THE MISSIONARY ATTITUDE

In Stage Three, the tensions between the outer and inner journeys increase. As a result of the intensity of this tension, those in this stage attempt to control and avoid the anxiety of uncertainty by seeking safety through identification with social and spiritual absolutes and dogmatism. Having failed to find happiness and self-fulfillment in self-absorption or in work, people look for a higher authority, which will answer their questions by telling them what to do to be a worthy person. They have begun to suspect that the answer to the question of their worth is within, but the pull of the world is still very strong. They decide that the answer lies in being a responsible, capable, hard-working, and giving person who performs actions that "matter" in the world. They seek the inner answer in the outer world by looking for it in religion, philanthropy, or a social cause. For the first time they really look outside themselves; and they see an inferior or broken spiritual or social world that needs correction and saving. To work hard at doing what they define as "good" becomes as important now as it was to work hard at earning a living.

Still seeing the world in extreme polarities of right/wrong and good/bad, they place tremendous focus and energy on doing what they feel is right to correct the wrong. This leads to rigid thinking and a need to control and manipulate to get the results they believe are absolutely necessary. Usually, in their intimate relationships, they expect their partners, friends, and children to adhere to their point of view. Ultimately, they cannot control the paths these others take. If the other person moves into more open stages of development or rebels against the rigidity, a crisis occurs, often resulting in a total breakdown in communication and relationship.

STATEMENT:
What is best for me is best for all.

CORE LEARNING:
Humility

SALIENT FEAR:
If I admit I don't have all the answers, I will be destroyed.

PRIMARY GIFT:
Social responsibility

TRANSITIONAL SHIFT:
Surrender of certainty for exploration

Persons moving into this stage often recall and relate to fantasies they had in early life in which they were the superior, strong, capable, all-knowing ones who saved others from harm. Psychologically, these people are calling upon a strong aspect of themselves to rescue the part of themselves that is vulnerable, hurting and whose survival is threatened. The fantasies are an attempt to heal their psyches while avoiding addressing psychological issues. In this stage, they search for their own healing while serving as rescuers of those in similar distress.

Some Stage Three people act out their fantasies in causes that rebel against or attempt to reform what they view as "the establishment," the current status quo, which in Stage Two they worked so hard to maintain.

As a young adult, I felt driven to take up the cause of the downtrodden, especially those neurologically handicapped and unhappy. In my fantasies, I was often Wonder Woman, bringing peace to warring nations. I was brave, wise, and could perform humanitarian miracles. There was no problem I could not solve with my wisdom and inner strength. In life, I hid my feelings of inadequacy with my competitiveness and drive to achieve, academically and professionally. I felt that if I followed the "rules," I would be safe and needed in the world.

Some Stage Three people act out their fantasies in causes that rebel against or attempt to reform what they view as "the establishment," the current *status quo*, which in Stage Two they worked so hard to maintain. Regardless of their arena, they view the world as broken and in need of major correction. They see others as underdeveloped, unenlightened, and incapable of saving or helping themselves.

Those in the Missionary Attitude stage offer many gifts to the world through their participation in good works and social action. Aware of the harm that comes from neglect and ignorance, they are willing to be active participants working for the economic, ecological, social, and educational good of humanity. They are agents of change who ensure that society at all levels is served and protected.

I first met Sarah in an Eskimo village located on Alaska's Kuskokwim River. Sarah and her husband, Roland, were missionaries assigned to teach Christianity to the natives of the area. At the time, I was part of a medical research project in which I traveled to villages along the Yukon and Kuskokwim Rivers and the Bering Sea.

Roland, a biologist by training, became a missionary after discovering an extreme emptiness in his life. Sarah had joined him in his ideals, hoping to discover the value of her life through her husband and their missionary work. They felt responsible for saving the souls of an ancient people who had survived spiritually and culturally for centuries. Sarah and Roland, both in their late twenties, did not express joy or enthusiasm for their work, yet they were certain their point of view was the correct one. The natives appeared to listen, but, when out of sight of the missionaries, they discussed the dilemma of having a belief sysem imposed.

Typical of others in this stage, Sarah and Roland had moved from ambivalence about their beliefs to certainty that their beliefs alone reflected the truth. Through an aura of innocence, their *personas* demonstrated a model, religious life dedicated to converting others to "right" beliefs.

Social and political activism provides another way for individuals to express the Missionary Attitude stage. Activists, fueled with intense emotions, channel their energy into doing constant battle against what they feel is morally wrong and for what they see as worthy causes. They are passionate people who care about outcome, certain of the rightness and morality of their positions. There are many battles to fight, worry about, and debate. There are many good things to save and many memories of wrongdoing to keep alive. They can devote themselves full time to being public defenders, using political and social arenas to repair what

Aware of the harm that comes from neglect and ignorance, they are willing to be active participants working for the economic, ecological, social, and educational good of humanity.

they feel is broken. Activists are modern warriors taking a we-against-them stance against a "big" enemy. To sustain an activist approach, one has to be willing to endure, if not relish, conflict and avoid discouragement. Many activists spend little time in reflection, rebounding quickly and continuing to fight the fight of their cause. Being outer directed, activists often sacrifice a personal life in order to focus their energies towards a social cause. Being an activist *is* life.

Ralph Nader, considered the activist of all activists, is well known for being faithful to his causes of consumer rights and safety, environmental protection, and governmental accountability. He has observed that young people who feel passionate about a cause tend to burn out after a few years. He views their interest in activism as a phase after which they move on to other ventures. His observation supports the view that activism reflects a stage of service that one can choose to either pass through or remain in for a lifetime.

They become absolutely certain about "right" cultural values, justice, and religious beliefs and strive to live a perfect, proper, and orderly life prescribed by both implicit and explicit rules.

PROCESS OF THE MISSIONARY ATTITUDE

STATE OF THE SELF

In an attempt to move out of the intense ambivalence of the second stage, people develop an extreme need to be in control. They become absolutely certain about "right" cultural values, justice, and religious beliefs and strive to live a perfect, proper, and orderly life prescribed by both implicit and explicit rules. Because their control is an attempt to balance their inner struggle with uncertainty, they become extremely sensitive about small problems and defeats that challenge their certainty. When challenged, they commonly tighten their control in defense and may become even more rigid in their thinking.

WORLD VIEW

Those in this stage see a world of duality with absolutes of right and wrong, good and bad, proper and improper. They are so certain of the rightness of their values and views that they have no qualms about imposing them onto others. Their attitude is one of "I am here to convince you of what I know is best for you and for everyone else in the world. Your life will be saved because of me."

They also hold a view that "my safety must be your safety; therefore, I must sacrifice myself for your benefit." This world view can serve as an impetus for activists to strive for change, especially if tragedy has impacted them in some way. Good often comes of this view because it raises social awareness and results in the enactment of protective regulations that serve the common good. As one example, the efforts of Mothers Against Drunk Driving have resulted in more stringent laws regarding driving while intoxicated. A second example is Sarah Brady, whose husband was shot during the attempted assassination of Ronald Reagan, and who has become a leading force in the passing of gun control bills.

RELATIONSHIP WITH GOD

Within a religious context, persons in this stage desire strict religious boundaries for validation and for emotional and spiritual safety. Fear of punishment characterizes their relationship with God. If not oriented toward religion, individuals tend to make a "god" of their political or social views. No matter what or who the god, Stage Three individuals develop or adopt clearly delineated rules,

Their attitude is one of "I am here to convince you of what I know is best for you and for everyone else in the world. Your life will be saved because of me."

values, and principles. The structure of this formal or informal dogma provides personal comfort and stability as well as a means of impacting the outside world. The belief is that behavior and standards must be regulated and restricted "for your own good." Because they see others as unenlightened and incapable, they feel justified in imposing and enforcing the "right way." When religious, those in this stage tend to be literal in their scriptural interpretations and not open to differing points of view. They feel they know what God wants and that it is their duty and responsibility to fulfill His request. To them, God is "out there" rather than within. Their prayer life is active, ritualized, and petitionary.

No matter what or who the god, Stage Three individuals develop or adopt clearly delineated rules, values, and principles.

Because those in this stage see others as wrong or ignorant and in need of saving, they can sacrifice their lives on behalf of others. They may have transcendent experiences in which they feel "called" in a deep, meaningful way to perform a specific mission in the world. When this occurs, their outer lives have a quality of unpredictability while their inner lives are ones of certainty of purpose.

Most religious individuals in this stage lead ordered and dry lives, minimizing surprises and unacceptable challenges. Their reasoning is very much in control and they are not open to receiving advice. For all the apparent surface harmony, however, a disquiet begins to undermine their certainties. This disquiet reveals itself in dryness in prayer and the inability to handle small problems and defeats.

Those whose "god" is social or political may actually thrive on conflict and chaos and find excitement in defending their opinions. The constant clamor of activity protects them from the dryness of their inner lives, and they may even experience fear when forced into solitude and quiet.

PREDOMINANT SHADOW ISSUES

The continuing search for outside validation of self-worth, especially from social causes and institutions, characterizes Stage Three. Sensitive to failure and fear of any contradiction of their reasoning, those in this stage do not want advice or to hear challenging points of view. They are unable to help themselves and tend not to accept help or consolation from others. They strive to meet their own rigid definition of a "good and responsible person," but feel overburdened by the misery of others and the problems in the world. They have difficulty shifting out of the belief that their job is to save others. They are so intent on the misery of others that they do not always recognize their own. They can remain in this darkness their entire lives, experiencing health and family problems because of the singleness of their focus.

The tendency to look to outer causes for their identity and to deny their darkness makes them vulnerable to numerous shadow issues. These shadow tendencies interfere with the flexibility and expansion of their thinking and behavior and the quality of their work and personal relationships.

Sensitive to failure and fear of any contradiction of their reasoning, those in this stage do not want advice or to hear challenging points of view.

PROJECTION

Caught in the polarity of right/wrong thinking, those in this stage project their shadow onto people, institutions, and causes that oppose their view. The psyche is in conflict whenever we deny, protest, or disclaim its dualistic nature. Robert Johnson's metaphor of the seesaw given in Chapter Four illustrates that any extreme will always reveal itself in the opposite behavior. Disowned and suppressed energy must go somewhere. Strong adherence to a right way is opposed by a desire to annihilate the wrong way.

By denying their darkness, those in Stage Three are vulnerable to acting out the shadow in "forbidden" areas of sex, power, and money. As Johnson explains, this is the psyche's attempt to rebalance its energies. Such persons or organizations may excessively punish or condemn anyone who acts out those traits they have forbidden in themselves. The Salem witch trials provide one example of this dichotomy.

Projection of power can also occur as a compensatory mechanism. In her autobiography, *A Desperate Passion*, activist Helen Caldicott explains that her activism against the use of nuclear power grew out of her powerlessness as a child. As an adult, she compensated for her feelings of powerlessness by confronting international politicians who had the power of endangering the future of children through their nuclear policies. She attempted to regain her personal power by rebelling against those she perceived as the world's most powerful.

The belief that "I have the answer, you don't" exemplifies pride enhanced by feelings of superiority. Proselytizing and rigid adherence to a point of view are overt expressions of pride. Pride gives birth to competition as different groups, each "right," compete with one another for converts, time, money, and attention.

Those in Stage Three fuel their causes with sentiment. Intense emotional energy colors their opinions and judgements. As such, they can impose their views onto others in an intrusive and dramatic way. This form of projection reflects the use of power to control others and leaves no room for negotiation or dialogue about differences. Those who are recipients of a communication from someone with a missionary attitude often feel an intrusion of their physical, mental, emotional, and spiritual boundaries.

Rigidity of thought accompanies attachment to form and outcome of service. Emotionally fed by the cause they espouse, they also become attached to those they serve, dependent on having a

Those who are recipients of a communication from someone with a missionary attitude often feel an intrusion of their physical, mental, emotional, and spiritual boundaries.

continual stream of people to save. Their strong tendencies toward martyrdom also lead them to encourage those they serve to
attach to them. In a sense, they must suffer at the hands of those
they serve in order to feel justified in their many sacrifices. Their
strong attachments fuel the use of power to manipulate and control others to do what they see as right.

DENIAL

Denial allows one to believe one is in control one's life.
Through denial one can simply avoid examining one's thinking,
behavior, values, and impact on others. Thinking in absolutes
represses one's own perspective as well as that of others. One
remains safe by remaining oblivious to the dualistic nature of the
human psyche.

People in this stage are often well-intentioned, but because
they resist expanding and deepening psychological and spiritual
knowledge, they often misdirect their service and are even incompetent. They deny the validity of the perspectives of those
they serve and, stuck in their point of view, do not develop true
compassion. Because they know they hold an attitude of being
superior and right, they may resist acquiring skills; this leads to
incompetence and serving at a level beyond their ability.

*People in this
stage are often
well-intentioned,
but because
they resist
expanding and
deepening
psychological
and spiritual
knowledge, they
often misdirect
their service and
are even
incompetent.*

NEGLECT

People having this intensity of inner control and rigidity experience great stress in their psyches. Through neglect of their
psychological well-being they can become physically and even
mentally ill. They may give to others to such a degree that they
fail to meet the needs of their families and themselves. For some,
the stress and sacrifice result in multiple health problems.

MODE OF SERVICE

Those in this stage desire to lead a "righteous life" and see service as an opportunity to convert people to the "right" way. Fearful of losing control, they tend not to help themselves and may find it difficult to accept the help of others. "In sum," writes St. Teresa, "I have found neither a way of consoling nor a cure for such persons other than to show them compassion in their affliction—and indeed, compassion is felt on seeing them subject to so much misery—and not contradict their reasoning."

They consider it a duty to follow an inner calling to contribute to the betterment of the world.

Persons in the Missionary Attitude stage often have a highly developed sense of **duty** as obligation from having integrated the work ethic into a responsible, "proper" life. They bring a well-developed **strong and skillful will** to their new focus on being responsible citizens and doing good in the world. They consider it a duty to follow an inner calling to contribute to the betterment of the world. Abiding by their rules and values, they practice **good will,** even willingly making personal sacrifices. For those in this stage, the definition of good will mirrors their overall rigidity, however, and their service usually limits rather than expands choice. If religiously oriented, they consider it a duty to participate in some form of spiritual practice.

Sometimes through a sense of duty rather than compassion, they tithe and make social contributions. Because they tend to hold an attitude of superiority and are attached to form and outcome, they cannot truly engage in **charity** as giving solely out of love for others. Instead, they place limitations on what they give and how they serve. They are motivated to do good as they see it. Their service is action-oriented and includes many charitable works and philanthropic endeavors, especially related to health, education, social needs, and social reforms. Because they feel compelled to participate in the greater good of humanity, those in the Missionary Attitude stage have a beginning awareness of a reality that transcends that of their own.

TRANSITIONING TO STAGE FOUR: THE WOUNDED HEALER

In the third stage the tensions between the outer and inner journeys increase and eventually reach a critical point. On the one hand, the person may have a regular prayer life and appear to lead a model religious and/or socially responsible life. On the other hand, ego-consciousness has gained an even firmer hold over the personality, and even this admirable life dedicated to saving others has become part of a *persona*.

To move on from this stage, individuals must release ego-control of what they believe a religious or socially responsible life is. This entails allowing the structure of their belief system to collapse when it no longer serves their spiritual journey. Determination to stay in this stage can lead to a deterioration of one's inner life that eventually erodes certainties and causes much misery. Some do not choose to move on and remain in this stage throughout their lives.

At the end of this stage, most can no longer deny that they experience life as laborious, burdensome, and stagnant. They can no longer tolerate the weight of their misery. They begin to suspect that their spiritual view is limited, that things are not as they seem, and that there must be a better way to live. They begin to suspect that this is not the end of the spiritual journey, that, in fact, they are still in spiritual "kindergarten." Now is the time to give up believing they know all the answers. Now is the time to surrender to exploring the unknown.

To move on from this stage, individuals must release ego-control of what they believe a religious or socially responsible life is.

The counterbalnce of pride is humility, and the learning of humility marks the end of this stage.

The counterbalance of pride is humility, and the learning of humility marks the end of this stage. With humility, one sees the limitations of one's thinking and way of life. Experiences of uncertainty and fears of failing or losing control force one to look elsewhere for self-worth. Not finding a sense of wholeness in institutions, religion, or social action in Stage Three, they continue their outward search in Stage Four by turning to relationships to meet their needs.

SUPPORT FOR STAGE THREE

As in Stage One and Two, those in Stage Three continue to look without rather than within for direction and well-being. While in Stage Three, they benefit only from support compatible with their beliefs regarding religion or social action. They feel most comfortable receiving help within their own community or group or from those with similar belief systems. They find practical, cognitive psychological help beneficial for purposes of problem solving, self-discovery, and, when needed, crisis management. Like those in Stage Two, they are people of action and accept educational and experiential opportunities to acquire, practice, and use their abilities and talents, if these do not challenge their views.

Persons in this stage need a different kind of support once they have acknowledged that their view of the world is exclusive and limited. This realization often generates an intense period of uncertainty, questioning, and giving up of control. Three major kinds of support are helpful for those bridging from Stage Three to Stage Four:

- help in letting go of their former beliefs without guilt and resentment,

- assistance in expanding their choices of other ways to be in the world, and

- integration of mind-body-spirit.

Personal exploration of ways to move out of a rigidly held point of view requires guidance and education about different psychological models of the human psyche, such as depth psychology and psychosynthesis. Through these approaches, the process of healing emotional wounds and developing healthy boundaries begins. Individuals in transition also need support in understanding the will and the impact of polarized attitudes on others. Once there is movement away from compartmentalization of life, the individual is ready to take initial steps towards integrating the physical, emotional, mental, and spiritual. Twelve-step programs offer acceptable alternatives to self-help and wholistic approaches.

Whether religiously oriented or not, those in this stage will find it helpful to question and contemplate their values and beliefs. They find it reassuring to learn from those who have moved beyond this stage into the next.

Personal exploration of ways to move out of a rigidly held point of view requires guidance and education about different psychological models of the human psyche, such as depth psychology and psychosynthesis.

*S*TAGE FOUR

The Wounded Healer

*B*y age eighteen I decided I wanted to live a life of selfless service. Throughout college and work life, I had multiple opportunities to serve. At age twenty-one I started the first speech pathology program for adults with aphasia in a nursing home. I moved to Alaska where I taught the deaf and worked with children and adults with brain injuries. Later, in San Francisco, I conducted research with those suffering brain trauma. At age thirty-three and for fourteen years thereafter, I served as a professor and first woman chairperson of a university medical sciences department.

No matter where I worked or in what capacity, I failed to experience the joy and happiness I expected from being of service. Why had the helping profession I had chosen resulted in an unfulfilling life? I thought I must need more schooling, more self-help groups, or a more responsible job. I began to suspect I had chosen my profession, not so much because of my concern for others, but because of my concern about my own psychology, neurology, and spirituality.

DESCRIPTION:
THE WOUNDED HEALER

Stage Four, the Wounded Healer, represents one final attempt to find meaning, purpose, and validation in the outside world. Instead of looking for happiness in materialism, work, causes, or institutions as in the first three stages, individuals search for meaning through personal and professional relationships. They move from serving a world that needs saving and correcting to serving with the hope of meeting their emotional needs. Outside appearances to the contrary, the Wounded Healer's underlying motivation for service is to be rescued rather than to rescue.

The primary characteristic of Wounded Healers is to give to others what they want for themselves. Their inner, often unconscious, belief is that "If I do this for others, it will happen for me." Many enter helping professions, marriage, and other partner relationships hoping to find a missing or lacking part within themselves. This creates personal and work relationships fraught with expectations and dependencies.

Characteristically, Wounded Healers also compartmentalize learning to a greater, more extreme degree than those in the first three stages. Wounded Healers apply what they have learned in one aspect of life but not in another. For example, a person may present an understanding and compassionate *persona* in the work place but be intolerant and unforgiving in the home. In going through the preceding evolutionary stages, the Wounded Healer accumulates vast knowledge and skill but has not yet integrated these in a way that impacts their daily lives. Even those who teach social, emotional, and spiritual skills do not incorporate what they teach into all aspects of their own lives.

Persons in this stage have internalized the work ethic, mastering methods and techniques and using their intellect in problem-

STATEMENT:
If I help others, I will get my emotional needs met.

CORE LEARNING:
Healthy boundaries

SALIENT FEAR:
I am not enough.

PRIMARY GIFT:
Generosity

TRANSITIONAL SHIFT:
Surrender of self-deception for self-responsibility

solving. They have taken an important step towards standing alone, not wanting others, work, or religion to define their worth. Yet they still look to relationships to make them whole and complete.

I moved into Stage Four in my early twenties when I became disillusioned with the strictness and rigidity of the church's teachings. I wanted to be independent and unrestrained by institutionally imposed restrictions. I sought to fulfill my life's mission by developing innovative training and service programs in private organizations that imposed fewer strictures and provided support for creativity. In each of my work situations, I did my best to do what I felt was right and good, hoping that eventually I would be happy and content with life. I stayed in the Wounded Healer stage for almost twenty-five years.

I began to realize that I was no Wonder Woman who could perform miracles and make everyone happy. I could not feel love and compassion for other people when I saw them as needing help; I hid from myself my own need to help them. My need to have them need me and to feel I could affect their lives arose from a superior/inferior viewpoint separating me from my own humanity and from that of others. On one hand, I experienced my life as rich with inspiration, energy, and creativity. On the other hand, I felt confused, bewildered, and at times overcome by sheer terror. I was not enough.

Crises caused by broken relationships, abandonment issues, loss of identity, betrayal, loss of financial security, and lack of achievement provide the necessary catalyst prompting Wounded Healers to examine the quality of their lives. They usually do not seek outside support until such a crisis occurs. If they choose not to seek support or do not have sufficient psychological strength to confront and work through a crisis, they usually continue to look outward for their validation. They either remain caught in their

The primary characteristic of Wounded Healers is to give to others what they want for themselves.

suffering or return to an earlier stage of awareness. They may become depressed and suicidal, particularly if they cannot see any viable choices.

The primary gift of those in Stage Four is their generosity. While seeking to meet their own needs through relationships, they endeavor to make a difference in the world by assisting others. They bring forward the gifts of the first three stages and are hard-working, competent, sensitive, and motivated to bring about constructive change in the health and well-being of others. They are socially and culturally conscious. They serve their communities. They care deeply about the well-being of humanity and are generous helpers in the world.

When I first met Christina, she was in her early forties and had worked as a therapist for twenty years. During that time, she had counseled hundreds of clients and led many therapy groups. Now she described herself as physically and mentally exhausted with "no more to give." She was also unable to leave an unhealthy relationship.

Christina's personal history made it clear she had selected a profession that related to her unmet emotional needs. She explained, "My family was very troubled. By the time I was ten years old, my mother had been hospitalized several times for depression, and my father stayed away from home and buried himself in his work. As a youngster, I became intrigued with psychology and wanted to help others. I looked to the field of psychology to provide me with insights and direction about my own overwhelming and bewildering emotions. I wanted to help others in situations similar to mine and so was trained to work with those having a history of emotional and physical abuse." Christina added that she had always wanted a romantic relationship that would give her a sense of being cared for physically and emotionally.

Crises caused by broken relationships, abandonment issues, loss of identity, betrayal, loss of financial security, and lack of achievement provide the necessary catalyst prompting Wounded Healers to examine the quality of their lives.

Instead, she repeatedly selected partners who were emotionally aloof and who did not benefit from her attempts to help them.

An imbalance between giving and receiving creates an obstruction in flow of the Life Force.

Christina's professional training focused exclusively on diagnosis and treatment based on the pathology of emotional and psychological health. Her training did not provide a framework for viewing a client wholistically from a comprehensive physical, mental, neurological, educational, and spiritual perspective. She counseled others solely through the window of their emotions. At no time did she consciously link her own emotional history and its needs and concerns with those of her clients. Christina admitted, "I have become good at what I do. People seem to gain value from my work with them. Yet I feel I give and give and gain nothing in return. I am becoming increasingly discouraged and distraught. I must need further education about newer and more effective methods."

With renewed enthusiasm, Christina began her study of other methods. She went back to school. She searched for answers that would help her understand the nature of the human mind and result in helping her clients and improving her own emotional state. Christina was in the Wounded Healer stage of awareness of service.

A similar phenomenon can occur within the family. Julianna, an established writer, once shared that she experienced the Wounded Healer stage early in her marriage to Ben. When she met Ben, he was a widower with two young children who was struggling to make a living and maintain a semblance of family life.

Recently divorced and at a career juncture, Julianna felt she could fill her emptiness and give her life definition by providing a stable home life for Ben and his children. She would find herself by saving them.

As time went on and the perfect picture of family did not

develop as planned, Julianna felt a tremendous sense of failure. Wounding herself by failing to meet her self-imposed expectations, she became depressed and felt unloved. She feared that if she could not meet their needs, she was nothing and had no reason to exist. Furthermore, she feared someone would discover she had failed. As she became more and more depressed, she projected her sense of failure outward, deciding that Ben and the children were at fault for not wanting to be helped.

An existential question emerges, "What is the true meaning of my life? Not, what did I think it was to be, but what is it truly?"

Julianna was in the fourth stage of awareness of service. Finally, feeling herself sliding into another cycle of depression, she realized she could choose to be responsible for her perceptions and feelings. With humility, she confronted her woundedness. Increasingly, Julianna accepted all parts of herself, the shadow and the light. As she opened toward herself, she also opened herself to her connection with the Absolute. She has subsequently continued her spiritual journey and has worked toward creating a healthy marriage and family life.

An imbalance between giving and receiving creates an obstruction in flow of the Life Force. This obstruction builds severe stress within the psyche, causing fragmentation. The psyche eventually collapses when it becomes so fragmented that it can no longer hold the strain of opposing energies. An identity crisis follows, involving the purpose and intent of the psyche itself. An existential question emerges, "What is the true meaning of my life? Not, what did I think it was to be, but what is it truly?"

PROCESS OF THE WOUNDED HEALER

STATE OF THE SELF

As in the Work Ethic and Missionary Attitude stages, Wounded Healers often lead well-ordered lives and are contributors to the community. Their view of life is physically, materially, and psychologically based. They develop *personas* that match social expectations of their roles as parents, professionals, coworkers, or partners in relationships. In the more private areas of their life, they are often fearful and despairing.

Having invested considerable time, energy, and money in searching to have their emotional needs met in personal and work relationships, they become greatly disillusioned when this does not happen.

Over time, tensions increase dramatically between the outer life and inner reality. Having invested considerable time, energy, and money in searching to have their emotional needs met in personal and work relationships, they become greatly disillusioned when this does not happen. Discovering the lack of meaning and purpose in their lives, they feel unworthy and experience self-hatred. They are vulnerable to having their views questioned or challenged because they lack a strong sense of self. Life is not what they thought it would be.

WORLD VIEW

During the first three stages, one has been building a world view aligned with certain outside standards. First, the world is chaotic and in need of ordering. Then, the world is ignorant and in need of correction. In Stage Three, the world is helpless and is need of saving. With these standards defining one's world view, one can relate to others through action and through wanting a world that is better for others than it has been for oneself. By Stage Four, individuals have discovered that the world they have seen so far has not fulfilled any of the emptiness or need for purpose they experience inside themselves. Still seeing a polarized world of we/they and right/wrong, they begin to believe that other people have answers they do not have and that they can get what these people have through relationship with them. The world becomes divided between those perceived as having full vessels and those perceived as having empty vessels.

RELATIONSHIP WITH GOD

This stage is a continuation of the attempt to find God in the outside world rather than within oneself. One looks to relationships, not to God, to meet one's needs. Wounded Healers have acknowledged that causes, institutions, and organized religion do not hold the answers to spiritual unfoldment; they now seek answers through psychology and relationships. Having taken a detour into relationships as a way to find meaning in life, they realize they remain spiritually unaware.

Those in this stage may yet return to their attachments to the physical and psychological worlds before finally committing to seeing life as a spiritual journey. They may also return to an earlier religious tradition, hoping that the spiritual journey will be easier if they do so. Vulnerable to looking to others to meet their spiritual needs, they can be susceptible to joining spiritual traditions or organizations with charismatic leaders who misuse power.

Because of the intensity of their emotional pain, prayer is important to Wounded Healers. Although prayers still tend to be petitionary in nature, they serve as a meaningful connection to God. Through this connection, they begin a search for another way to view themselves and their relationship to God.

PREDOMINANT SHADOW ISSUES

Shadow issues of Wounded Healers involve repeated attempts to seek psychological completion through relationship. Because they have difficulty differentiating their own needs from the needs of others, they become enmeshed in the physical and psychological boundaries of others, not knowing where they end and the other person begins.

The world becomes divided between those perceived as having full vessels and those perceived as having empty vessels.

PROJECTION

Wounded Healers frequently misuse personal power by intruding on the boundaries of others. They do this by projecting onto others what they believe to be missing within themselves. In this way they give responsibility for their feelings and emotions to others, thereby abdicating self-responsibility and personal power. In doing this, they exemplify their belief that "You have what I don't have. Therefore, I can get what I don't have from you." When the other person fails to give them what they want, they feel betrayed and abandoned. Rather than recognizing that they have actually rejected their inner strength, they blame the other person. This blame usually takes the form of anger and demand for change.

Because they have difficulty differentiating their own needs from the needs of others, they become enmeshed in the physical and psychological boundaries of others, not knowing where they end and the other person begins.

Wounded Healers are attached to the belief that happiness lies in relationships. They are certain that relationships will provide them with what they need if only they find the right one. They become attached to a never-ending search for the perfect friend, partner, coworker, or spouse. They are attached to their concept of what a relationship should look like, which often involves exclusivity and expectations of certain behaviors. Once they find someone who seems to meet their criteria, they might become possessive and demanding.

Another way Wounded Healers abdicate personal power is by believing that "If I give you the nurturance and support I need, I will meet my own need for nurturance and support." This is giving to get. Because they have exaggerated expectations of what they should receive in return, others can rarely meet their needs. When this disappointment occurs, the giver feels drained, disillusioned, and angry.

Because they experience their own needs as being met through their focus on the needs of others, they defend against receiving help. They see themselves as needing only to give and not to receive. Additionally, because of their need to be needed and therefore to be the giver, they do not recognize the gifts of others. By the end of this stage, Wounded Healers have fully developed this *persona* or way of presenting themselves in the world.

DENIAL

Wounded Healers are caring and responsible people who dedicate themselves to helping others while evading the need to attend to their own inner work. They therefore serve through the veil of their "unfinished business"—all that is incomplete, unfaced, and unacknowledged within themselves. Their denial is often so great that they live in fear that others will see their inner state or will discover the facts of their personal history. To hide themselves from themselves and from the world, they erect barriers by being in control of the results of their work and in charge of the lives of others. They earnestly believe they can bypass their inner work on behalf of the needs of others, as though they are exempt from or beyond the consequences of their own unresolved emotional pain.

Wounded Healers are willing to see service as having educational and human advantages in that it provides opportunities to learn from and about others. They expect others, however, to do what they themselves have not done: integrate intellectual knowledge and experiential wisdom into daily life. Their level of willingness and ability to apply what they learn in their own lives determines the competence of their service. By not engaging in their own inner work, they limit the potential for healing in those they serve. One can support another's potential for healing only if one experiences that potential within oneself. One would not seek support for addictions, for example, from someone who

Because they experience their own needs as being met through their focus on the needs of others, they defend against receiving help.

has not faced and to some degree healed the cause of his own addictions. Wounded Healers tend to teach what they *need* to learn rather than what they *have* learned.

NEGLECT

The gap between knowledge and its application eventually becomes so great that Wounded Healers may experience the mental and physical exhaustion of burnout. Burnout often leads to an existential crisis in which one questions the quality, integrity, and meaning of life. Wounded Healers recognize they can no longer continue the neglect of their own well-being while in relationship with others or while in service.

MODE OF SERVICE

Wounded Healers have a strong sense of **duty** and responsibility towards others and are willing to set themselves aside for the good of family and community. Through discipline, they reach their personal and work goals through well-developed strong, skillful, and good will. Values, ethics, and standards are important to them.

On Maimonides' continuum of giving, Wounded Healers commonly give significantly before being asked. They also give without knowing to whom they are giving, although they want recipients to know their identity. Acknowledgment and appreciation of their giving meet the Wounded Healer's emotional needs.

Wounded Healers willingly engage in good works and often expand their work to a global level. They feel a deep connection with all beings, sentient and insentient. To them, life itself is about giving, loving, and doing. Their *dharma* is to practice peace and service in the world. They expand their sense of duty to include a spiritual practice and an active devotional life.

They expect others, however, to do what they themselves have not done: integrate intellectual knowledge and experiential wisdom into daily life.

Wounded Healers practice **charity** as an expression of compassion and unconditional love. Sensitive to the needs and suffering of others, they attempt to provide quality service. They willingly involve themselves personally with those they serve. Through facing the suffering of others, they begin to face their own attitudes about suffering. They turn caring for others into action. They strive to give the right thing in the right amount at the right time and for the right reason.

To them, life itself is about giving, loving, and doing.

TRANSITIONING TO STAGE FIVE: HEALING THE HEALER

The discovery that one can never receive self-validation through a relationship with another person can be so emotionally devastating it results in feelings of abandonment by the world and by God. Typically, a significant loss in life, such as loss of health, job, spouse, or other family member, triggers this realization. The ensuing crisis propels one into considerable emotional distress, confusion, and perplexity, especially if one resists the process of new growth. The outside world offers no relief to the pain; nothing and no one has answers. A struggle ensues between believing and not believing that true strength arises from within. Withdrawing projections and taking responsibility for them requires confrontation of hidden emotional pain.

The transition to Stage Five typically occurs between the ages of thirty-five and fifty as a significant crisis of personal identity and life purpose. This crisis signals a psychological and spiritual readiness to redirect outwardly focused energies inward. To achieve this change, the old must crumble and the new must be built. An intense inner upheaval and disorientation accompanied by a sense of urgency characterizes this death and rebirthing process.

The realization that they have thoroughly exhausted all pos-

The transition to Stage Five typically occurs between the ages of thirty-five and fifty as a significant crisis of personal identity and life purpose.

sibility of finding resolution and contentment outside themselves accompanies this Stage Four crisis. Because identification with and attachment to the body, the material world, and relationships are so strong, they have great difficulty accepting without question that their true strength lies within. Initially, this truth may induce the fear of the unknown enhanced by the mistaken belief that it means they must withdraw from the world, leaving behind all they love. At this point some people experience being frozen by two questions: "Who will I be?" *and* "More importantly, who will be with me?" They find comfort in knowing that living from a place of inner strength means staying in the world while expressing the depth and richness of shared humanity.

Basically, this particular identity crisis occurs because of intense inner conflict created by the widening gap between the knowledge known and the knowledge applied. "I know that and will use what I know" opposes "I know that and I will not use what I know." The psyche becomes severely stressed by the demand to keep such extremely disparate energies in place because its natural inclination is to move towards balance and wholeness without ambivalence. Most people experience the psychic stress as physical and mental exhaustion and as depression.

Out of their fear of the unknown, Wounded Healers desperately try to maintain the stability of their lives. This approach creates more inner conflict and outer stress. They finally reach a point where their inability to control the chaos of circumstances humbles them into a sincere quest. At this point, they are willing to begin examining the quality and integrity of their inner and outer lives and ponder their purpose and mission.

Because they need considerable energy to do the necessary inner work to bring about this transformational change, they often require temporary retreat from the outer world. Focusing inward means reviewing one's life, exploring options, questioning beliefs, and allowing the healing process to unfold. Patiently, through this process, they commit to the unknown, to wholeness, and to the integration of the physical, mental, emotional, and spiritual parts of the self. Finally, they recognize and accept the self-deception of trying to meet their needs through work or institutions or personal and professional relationships.

Willingness instigates and fuels this venture into the unknown. Only as they are willing to surrender the need to control are they free to explore another way to live in the world. They break free from conditioning and begin to question every belief and attitude as they become responsible for what they think, do, and say.

Whether or not they consciously recognize it, the impetus to change is a direct reflection of the soul's readiness to reveal more of its true destiny. Attaining self-responsibility for their actions and reactions leads to inner freedom and gives the gift of conscious choice. Rather than being buffeted by life circumstances, they can choose to use them as opportunities to learn and grow. As they learn about the soul's true nature, they awaken to their destiny. They become vibrantly and enthusiastically alive.

To move out of the Wounded Healer stage, one must allow this preconceived structure of one's personal world to collapse. That world view is no longer compatible with one's emotional and spiritual evolution. Rather than look to the world to give one security, confidence, and equanimity, one begins to look within. The world view now must be undone if the new is to emerge.

During this time, every belief about the meaning of life stands ready for review and challenge. Their denial will be exposed to themselves and others. All hidden motivations for service must be examined and corrected. Afraid of losing control and out of

Whether or not they consciously recognize it, the impetus to change is a direct reflection of the soul's readiness to reveal more of its true destiny.

pride, they can initially resist finding and accepting help from others. Humility finally allows them to acknowledge their neglect of spiritual development and to connect to their inner strength.

During this time, every belief about the meaning of life stands ready for review and challenge.

SUPPORT FOR STAGE FOUR

Those who pass through the Wounded Healer stage are ready to seriously begin their inner work. An intense period of personal growth and healing begins. They now make a commitment to their wholeness, the integration of all parts of self—physical, mental, emotional, and spiritual. Transpersonal psychological approaches, including depth psychology, psychosynthesis, metaphysics, and mind-body-spirit disciplines, are useful as are wholistic and alternative approaches. It is helpful to refer to philosophical and psychological frameworks when questioning and contemplating one's beliefs. This includes exploring a deeper spiritual dimension to life within both Eastern and Western traditions. It also includes recognizing the many gifts in their lives and their shadow's hidden potentials awaiting realization.

Individuals in this powerful time of transition benefit from an in-depth examination of their personal and work relationships. Three major kinds of support are helpful in bridging from Stage Four to Stage Five:

- supportive exploration of co-dependency and boundary issues,

- support and direction while accepting the self-deception they have engaged in using relationships to meet their emotional needs, and

- ongoing support in inner healing work as they

  - explore options

- question lifelong beliefs by reviewing their lives and their motivations for choosing their work, and

- allow the healing process to unfold as they identify areas of unfinished business.

Cultivating willingness and patience is important because of the depth and breadth of self-examination and inner work that lie ahead. For purposes of encouragement and co-sharing of information and experience, individuals profit from being in the company of others engaged in a similar transition.

Cultivating willingness and patience is important because of the depth and breadth of self-examination and inner work that lie ahead.

Stage Five

Healing the Healer

In 1976, I made a pilgrimage to Moscow to meet my mentor in neuropsy-chology, Alexander Luria. Through him I hoped to find the "soul" I searched for in my work. Political interference had disrupted the work of this gifted clinician for years. Yet, he had found a way to serve by writing about his work in a way that brought comfort and benefit to many.

As I waited on the bus for permission to enter his institute, I heard his voice within me say, "It doesn't matter what you do as long as you come from the heart."

In 1979, after twenty-five years as a helping professional, I became des-perate to find joy in serving others. I stopped working and went on a six-month quest to discover "what it means to serve through God's eyes." Wherever I traveled, I contacted a service organization and asked to serve them in what-ever way they needed.

In the process of this journey, I learned a very important lesson—being of service meant doing whatever needed to be done with no attachment to the form of the task and with no investment in its outcome. I have also learned there is an integral relationship between service and my own personal healing process.

To come from my heart and to serve through God's eyes means exploring and deepening my understanding of the relationship of self and service from a spiritual perspective. Since 1980, this has been the primary focus of my work at the Institute for Attitudinal Studies.

DESCRIPTION:
HEALING THE HEALER

The Healing the Healer Stage of awareness begins the second phase of the individuation process. This stage marks a clear transition on the spiritual journey. Knowing events and relationships mirror their inner reality, Stage Five individuals become increasingly aware of the power of thoughts, beliefs, and choices. No longer searching outside themselves for their right "to be," they turn inward and begin the journey of actualizing the soul's destiny.

Those in this stage bring with them the learning, accomplishments, and skills they have gathered thus far, while at the same time leaving behind their old way of viewing their place and their service in the world. Fully satisfied that the road home cannot be found in the material world, they say good-bye to what their life has been. The uncharted territory of their psychological and spiritual natures lies before them. They are about to discover a new foundation for a way of being and serving in the world; this foundation may take decades and even lifetimes to fully manifest in their human lives.

I began the earliest part of my journey into the Healing the Healer stage in 1973 when I confronted the vastness of the neglect of my emotional and spiritual self. I began to immerse myself in various metaphysical teachings, personal growth approaches, and psychotherapeutic traditions. Over time, I saw that I could choose not to be a victim of circumstances. I could meet my emotional and spiritual needs from within myself. I heard others' calls for help as my own. I became aware of the law of synchronicity bringing other people, events, and me together at the right time and place for mutual learning. I also began to notice the law of

STATEMENT:
The way out is the way in.

CORE LEARNING:
Willingness

SALIENT FEAR:
I'll never achieve my goal.

PRIMARY GIFT:
Authenticity

TRANSITIONAL SHIFT:
Surrender of knowing to not knowing

extension at work as I naturally extended my inner healing to others and watched others do the same for me. As I focused on my inner work, obstacles to my personal growth began to fall away. I began to see much that I had denied within myself, related to both my fears and my divinity.

To serve in the stage of Healing the Healer necessitates a shift of one's mind from an outer focus to inner contemplation.

I realized that every time I compared myself to another person in any way, I built a wall of separation between us. By claiming health, fortune, and wholeness as my rightful inheritance, I claimed them as the common heritage I shared with each person. By acknowledging our commonality, I could then join with another person in experiencing Divine Love.

In 1986, I moved deeper still into Stage Five by making a conscious commitment to expand my understanding of this stage while working within the context of an educational and spiritual service organization. Clearly, this commitment has required self-effort, discipline, and practice.

To serve in the stage of Healing the Healer necessitates a shift of one's mind from an outer focus to inner contemplation. Servers address the status of their inner being instead of continuing to believe their problems are outside themselves. They see those they serve as capable of doing the same and support them in finding answers within themselves.

One of the major gifts of people in this stage is their willingness to use life as a classroom with unlimited opportunities to heal and be healed. They view their lives as a way to learn about themselves and to deepen their understanding of others. To them, every interaction is an opportunity to look within to find both obstacles and strengths for their spiritual evolution. They view their relationships as true partnerships and acknowledge the beauty of the inner soul.

When Christina, whose Wounded Healer story I shared in the last chapter, began her inner work, I observed a shift in the way that she served others. She realized she did not need to change her vocation as a "helper"; she needed to change her inner attitude about her role. She saw that assisting others had less to do with what she did and more to do with her state of mind as she did it. She noticed that her clients reflected her own areas of unfinished business. Whenever she reacted instead of responding to someone's behavior, she saw it as a "red flag" to turn within. She initiated a search for the hidden parts of herself that prevented her from experiencing equanimity in the moment. Christina had moved to the fifth stage of awareness of service.

The fifth stage is a long process because it involves undoing the belief system of the previous four stages.

The fifth stage is a long process because it involves undoing the belief system of the previous four stages. At its onset, persons reclaim parts of themselves that have been scattered about and begin to work with the concept of self-responsibility. They develop an awareness of the Witness Self, the capacity to observe oneself without judgement, and a proficiency in self-inquiry. They are willing to look within and discover obstacles to the awareness of their true nature. As they move deeper into this stage, they gradually become self-accountable without guilt or shame.

Their vision moves out of duality, from one of exclusion or either/or to one of inclusion or both/and. They experience a shorter recovery time when they make a mistake. They develop a sensitivity to energy and learn how to use double vision, the ability to see the reality of a situation while simultaneously seeing beyond it to its spiritual essence. They value integrity and are positive and uplifting. The ego resists growth, and sometimes they feel like stopping the process. At such times, they may become ambivalent and can move back into crisis. They must maintain vigilance until gradually they attain mastery of the personal will and can surrender to Divine Will.

PROCESS OF HEALING THE HEALER

STATE OF THE SELF

One knows that true strength lies within and that true validation is self-validation.

In this stage, individuals begin in earnest to allow the *persona*-identification to crack and ego-consciousness to release total control of the psyche. A new, more powerful center begins to emerge that calls attention to itself and demands a response. There is a certainty now about the self, a sense of validity, of self-strength. One knows that true strength lies within and that true validation is self-validation. Stage Five people move beyond a purely personal God and are able to comprehend the Absolute Unknowable. Looking inward, they begin to approach the depths of the True Self. Through absorption in the Absolute, peace comes to the soul.

WORLD VIEW

The learning from previous stages integrates into a new world view. All along, the individual has been learning how to move from restriction to freedom, from certainty to uncertainty, from knowing to unknowing, from outer to inner. Prior stages have strengthened the person's ego-consciousness and the *persona* until she finally discovers where God does not reside. Explorations of all possibilities in the outside world are necessary before giving up investment in the world. Not to so explore impedes the ability to focus one's attention inward while living in the world.

The awakening-within-to-Spirit is powerfully present now and influences the way people view the world. They experience the world as a classroom in which to learn and grow spiritually and to become aware of their true inner reality. Attention to one's inner state requires responsibility for one's choices. This is how individuals change both in world view and level of service. At this point, they understand that one can only choose one's own beliefs and attitudes; one cannot choose for another. Taking responsibility for the consequences of past choices requires not only honesty but self-compassion.

RELATIONSHIP WITH GOD

This stage involves the joining of personal will with Divine Will through the Transpersonal Will. Individuals are souls with personalities having unique qualities and inclinations. As a result, they differ in life purpose and expression of service. Alignment with Divine Will reveals to each the uniqueness of the individual soul's plan. Such alignment also generates the inspiration and energy necessary to express the soul's destiny, its individual spiritual assignment. Without this alignment, people cannot be the joyful, spontaneous, and grateful instruments of the Divine Plan that they are intended to be.

More and more is asked of individuals as they proceed on the spiritual journey. The hand of the Absolute is ever extending and Its call never ceases. Old habit patterns based on beliefs in the material world continue to demand attention; therefore, individuals need to apply great self-effort to succeed in lifting a finger to meet God's. They require spiritual discipline to ensure a quiet mind through which to hear Divine Will and to generate the inner strength to follow its guidance. The harmony between inner and outer realities is now a possibility, although they must remain

Old habit patterns based on beliefs in the material world continue to demand attention; therefore, individuals need to apply great self-effort to succeed in lifting a finger to meet God's.

mindful of the need to remember to watch through the eyes of the Witness Self and to listen with their inner ears.

Carl Jung said, "Among all my patients in the second half of life—that is to say, over thirty-five—there has not been one whose problem in the last resort was not that of finding a religious outlook on life. It is safe to say that every one of them fell ill because he had lost what the living religions of every age have given to their followers, and none of them has been really healed who did not regain his religious outlook." The physical, psychological, and spiritual journeys now integrate and become one.

The physical, psychological, and spiritual journeys now integrate and become one.

Once individuals make the commitment to respond to the call to move inward, they recognize when the world tempts them outward again. Continuing their journey inward seems supported by the inner call itself. As St. Teresa explained, "Once the great King, who is in the center dwelling place of this castle, sees their good will, He desires in His wonderful mercy to bring them back to Him. Like a good shepherd, with a whistle so gentle that even they themselves almost fail to hear it, He makes them recognize His voice and stops them from going so far astray and brings them back to their dwelling place. And this shepherd's whistle has such power that they abandon the exterior things in which they were estranged from Him and enter the castle."

PREDOMINANT SHADOW ISSUES

When moving inward, one comes face-to-face with the unseen parts of oneself. Persons experience the "dark night of the soul" as they challenge the forces that oppose their going inward. "Dark" forces are those parts of inner reality that resist growth and spiritual unfoldment. Within the psyche, a place exists where the natural and supernatural join, where the dark and the light meet. This is the place of choice, the fulcrum of the shadow's seesaw where creative synthesis resolves seeming polarities.

To serve the highest good possible in any given set of circumstances, individuals in this stage must practice continuous inner work centered on the purification and integration of the shadow. Continuous inner work provides the only way to address the denied parts of oneself through which one habitually has served. By removing the veil of unfinished business, one opens the way for Divine Will to manifest. The fruit of this unceasing inner work matures into deepened compassion for self and others.

PROJECTION

Stage Five primarily focuses on recognition, acceptance, and becoming responsible for projections. Most of the projections relate to pride and power. The emergent understanding of their spiritual nature tempts unhealed healers to spiritual pride. Spiritual pride includes the belief that one has special powers, qualities, and talents that others do not have and the belief that one has the power to give these qualities and talents to others. From a place of spiritual pride, unhealed healers project pity and weakness onto others, failing to see other peoples' inner strengths.

Unstable in their understanding of the true source of being, unhealed healers believe that others have the power to steal both their peace of mind and Divine Love Itself. They are not secure in the power to choose how they feel or react.

A major challenge in this stage is to surrender personal power to Divine Power. Unhealed healers are attached to the outcome of their service and want to make it happen. They believe they can determine the what, how, and when of their service. This attachment to control, to attempt to be the cause of things, is

To serve the highest good possible in any given set of circumstances, individuals in this stage must practice continuous inner work centered on the purification and integration of the shadow.

deeply rooted in human nature. Relinquishing it requires accepting and trusting a higher plan. By controlling either the form of
service or its outcome, an individual limits the spirit of the service, restraining it from its highest expression.

DENIAL AND NEGLECT

People in this stage use every encounter as service, and every service as a reflection of their inner state.

The desire to believe that their new awareness has healed them
often leads unhealed healers to deny what remains unhealed. They
then project this denial through an attitude of "I have the power
to heal others and the world." They know the answers lie within,
but have not integrated this knowledge in a way that fully releases
the belief that problems are outside in the world.

Unhealed healers deny their own inner power and that of others. Fear then arises that others will take their personal power
away from them. As they surrender their need for external power,
they awaken to their inner power, accepting their own and others'
personal strengths and potential.

As they progress, they become impatient for the rewards of
their endurance and hard work. Moments of enlightenment and
transformation may alternate with feelings of discouragement, self-
doubt, and self-pity. Now that they see that the way out is in and
are acquiring the skills to take themselves there, they want the
process to advance more quickly.

Inner work requires taking responsibility for perceptions and
choices and for one's mental and physical health. As unhealed
healers progress, neglect becomes less and less an issue. They strive
for a balanced life.

MODE OF SERVICE

The choice to use each encounter for the single purpose of
seeing in each person all that one has not forgiven in oneself marks

the transition to the Healing the Healer stage. The more one focuses on one's inner state, the less one is attached to the form or action of service. People in this stage use every encounter as service, and every service as a reflection of their inner state. Through this process, they understand that their state of mind is the foundation of their service. Therefore, translating service into action provides a specific context in which to learn to monitor their inner state. They view **duty** as the container of life, an expression of personal *dharma* and its connection to Eternal *Dharma*. It is not what we do in the world that matters but the inner attitude with which we do it. When the person fully understands the truth of this statement, all service becomes true charity, an extension of unconditional love.

It is not what we do in the world that matters but the inner attitude with which we do it.

Persons in this stage are aware of the evolutionary shifts of service and recognize the many ways the laws of service operate in their own and others' lives. From the understanding that service is about the inner state of the server, individuals become more conscious of how they serve and are served. They become self-responsible in the helping relationship. They recognize the interconnection of their minds with the minds of others and see the helping relationship as a dynamic and equal partnership between server and served. Service takes on a new spirit and is more about "being" than about "doing." Because they are knowledgeable about the ways to uproot the cause of suffering and thereby eliminate suffering, they represent the third noble truth of Buddhism called the "cessation of suffering."

In this stage, individuals learn to use double vision—the ability to see both the behavior *and* beyond the behavior. They apply double vision to themselves and to others. In this way, they acknowledge the true reality of Divine Love as they support another's personal growth process. Rather than using the will to control their relationships, they refocus their intention inward and align their will with Divine Will. They accept that given their limited spiritual vision they cannot know the nature of the greatest good for themselves or for others. Their alignment with Divine Will through the **Transpersonal Will** enables them to practice true **charity**, giving the right thing in the right amount at the right time for the right reason.

To evolve to their highest possible level, they are patient, gentle, and unconditionally accepting of their own healing and learning. Their attitudes create the expanded psychological and spiritual space necessary to allow others to choose other ways of being. Because they do not impose expectations on others, those they serve have nothing to resist and are free to be themselves. Their inner state reflects the steadiness and wisdom of Absolute Reality. Their presence can act to remind those they serve of that reality within themselves. In this way, the servers serve others solely by the quality of their inner state.

Those in Stage Five serve within a framework of three guidelines:

- creating a safe emotional environment,
- honoring the process, and
- staying on purpose.

They **create a safe emotional space** for another by allowing the person to share deep personal feelings without fear of betrayal, shame, or lack of confidentiality. To create this environment, a server must be willing to set aside his own emotional needs in order to be fully present. Good eye contact and refraining from interjecting personal stories, giving advice, or making interpretations communicate this willingness. The server actively participates in his own emotional healing process and

Those in Stage Five serve within a framework of three guidelines:
- *creating a safe emotional environment,*
- *honoring the process, and*
- *staying on purpose.*

monitors the condition of his own mind. To create a safe place, the server:

- applies double vision, acknowledging the presented situation while seeing beyond it,

- uses intuition and inner wisdom for guidance,

- shares personal experiences only if doing so supports the one served, and

- encourages open and honest communication.

The server is also aware that to provide a safe space for someone else to work on an issue like anger, death, or betrayal he himself must feel safe with the issue.

Honoring the process requires trusting that the healing process will unfold according to a higher plan. To honor the process the server:

- encourages the person to listen to her own inner wisdom,

- detaches from any expectations about outcome,

- allows the person to take responsibility for her own choices,

- makes no assumptions about the person's experiences or perceptions, and

- refrains from evaluation or judgement of the person's actions and choices.

Staying on purpose is a way of creating comfortable boundaries for a relationship and a situation. The server takes responsibility for remembering that every interaction is an opportunity to practice peace, to forgive self and others, and to extend love. With this as the server's intent, the server and served focus on a specific, mutually agreed upon task or issue. To stay on purpose, the server:

The server takes responsibility for remembering that every interaction is an opportunity to practice peace, to forgive self and others, and to extend love.

- assists the person in finding her own answers,

- remembers that server and served are students and teachers for one another, and

- keeps the interaction focused on the intent of the supportive relationship.

By understanding service as an altar of devotion, servers increasingly take responsibility for their perceptions and choices and hold the reality of the presence of Divine Love within themselves and others.

To Healed Healers, service becomes a means of **purification**, providing opportunities for removing the obstacles to inner peace. They recognize that others serve them by mirroring the quality of their inner state. They view reactions as projections and as motivators for doing inner work. During this time, they may reexperience reverting to behaviors or beliefs they had thought healed. These experiences and "dark nights" of questioning or feeling abandoned by God are part of the purification process.

Through their relationships with others, Stage Five individuals apply and deepen what they have learned from their inner work. They serve and are served by others. Others reflect back to them the nature and quality of their inner state, aspects of their unfinished business, and reminders of the reality of Divine Love. This mutuality of service is essential for their emotional and spiritual well-being.

At this stage, service begins to be an **altar of devotion**. The individual feels the first inkling of the oneness of *doing* and *being*, of acting *in* the world while not being *of* it, of loving others, and of the bliss of love for the Absolute. The goals when serving others are to listen to the Inner Voice, to see the inner strength and rich resources of others, and to have no expectations of outcome. By understanding service as an altar of devotion, servers increasingly take responsibility for their perceptions and choices and hold the reality of the presence of Divine Love within themselves and others. As they heal, they become capable of responding to others with understanding and compassion.

TRANSITIONING TO STAGE SIX: SELFLESS ACTION

The final steps in Stage Five require experiencing one's connection to Divine Love and being willing to share that love with others. Only when one thoroughly lives and practices the lessons of Stage Five is one prepared to move into the Sixth Stage.

Viewing life from a cohesive philosophical framework assists in guiding anyone through significant changes. A philosophical framework provides knowledge about a certain subject and offers ways to practice that knowledge. The Universal Laws of Service explained in Chapter One and the Universal Tributes given here provide the philosophical framework for integrating the knowledge one knows with its application in daily life. Using this framework is a way to learn and practice self-responsibility for thoughts, actions, and words. The Universal Laws of Service and the Ten Universal Tributes are guides for actualizing the unity of personal healing and service.

The Universal Laws of Service and the Ten Universal Tributes are guides for actualizing the unity of personal healing and service.

The Ten Universal Tributes and their Tenets teach specifically how to manifest the Laws of Service in one's life. The Tributes show how to shift thoughts, actions, and words in order to look within rather than without for wholeness. In this way, the Ten Universal Tributes provide a road map for becoming self-responsible.

Each Tribute addresses the quality of the inner state of the server and the relationship of the server's inner state to the quality of service. The word "tribute" describes the intentionality or quality of one person's relationship with another person. Being in the presence of another human being and having an opportunity to serve them is a tribute, a gift. In giving a tribute, one holds all one gives, says, or does in a spirit of gratitude, respect, and honor.

In moving from Stage Five into Stage Six, identifying, apply-

In moving from Stage Five into Stage Six, identifying, applying, and integrating the knowledge and spirit inherent in the Universal Laws of Service and the Ten Universal Tributes support one's psychological and spiritual development.

ing, and integrating the knowledge and spirit inherent in the Universal Laws of Service and the Ten Universal Tributes support one's psychological and spiritual development. A sense of purposefulness emerges, providing sustenance through the ebb and flow of life, individually and collectively. Specific practices, such as contemplation, self-inquiry, meditation, journaling, imagery, and emotional/mental exercises, support this actualization process.

**My life goal is to align my will with Divine Will
and to increase the time I function in
this state of Higher Knowing.**

TRIBUTE
ONE

TENETS

1. *Universal Will expresses Itself through my Transpersonal Will to my personal will; in this way, my life purpose and mission are manifestations of the Divine.*

2. *The clarity of the expression of Divine Will through my personal will is dependent upon my willingness to develop and strengthen my will through inner work.*

3. *Experiences of synchronicity and an increased sense of inner well-being provide feedback that Divine Will is expressing itself through my personal will.*

4. *Because the energy and skill of the will are neutral and can be used for good or for harm, I am responsible for learning to use my will in a beneficent way.*

5. *The Witness Self and the will form the center of my consciousness; the Witness Self passively observes and the will actively selects, initiates, directs, or inhibits my thoughts, feelings, and actions.*

6. *Failure to develop and strengthen my will leads to a sense of meaninglessness and mental inertia and loss of the ability to make decisions and changes and to recognize and act upon intuition.*

7. *Continually developing and exercising the will throughout my lifetime leads to increased inner strength and greater certainty of my connection with the Divine when faced with challenges and responsibilities and when serving others.*

8. *A psychologically and spiritually healthy will selects, initiates, and carries out actions that serve the psychological and spiritual well-being of self and others.*

TRIBUTE TWO

I know my chosen life's purpose is in alignment with a Higher Purpose for me when I am inspired and when I experience the joy, spontaneity, and gratitude of service.

TENETS

1. To live life fully, I ask myself in every moment: Why am I here? How am I to be? What am I to do? Who am I to do this with? Where am I to go?

2. I have been given a unique assignment by the Divine and, having accepted this function, I live my life with integrity, commitment, and gratitude.

3. When I am out of harmony with the Divine's purpose for me, I become attached to the material world and its tangible rewards.

4. To be inspired is to put the Divine first in my life, thereby aligning my will with Divine Will and fulfilling my assigned life purpose and mission.

5. To inspire is to be inspired.

6. The energy of the Divine is spontaneous because it is only in the moment that the highest good can be served.

7. It is not what I do in my life that matters but the love, joy, and gratitude with which I do it.

8. Experiences throughout my life, even when seemingly inconsequential, serve as stepping stones to the eventual fulfillment of my chosen life purpose.

*Divine Will works through me as me
when I have no attachment to the form of the task
and no expectations of outcome.*

TRIBUTE THREE

TENETS

1. The manner, style, and form of my service is unique to me because the Divine expresses Itself through the personality.

2. The "me" that the Divine works through reflects a soul engaged in a certain stage of spiritual unfoldment; this "me" has a unique psychological and spiritual history, both consciously and unconsciously lived.

3. I cannot decide for others what or how they use what is offered to them.

4. The level of my service is limited by identification with the suffering of others and by attachment to my beliefs and to the material world.

5. I am here solely to offer my service to others with the purest inner motivation possible.

6. When I offer service with no expectations of return or outcome, I simultaneously offer a psychological space in which the receiver can see and accept what is best for them in that moment.

7. No direct correlation exists between the form of service and the level of service; therefore, the highest level of service can be expressed in any action.

8. The quality of service offered is dependent upon the nature of the inner state of the one who serves; I need do nothing and yet perform the highest service.

TRIBUTE FOUR

By continually doing my inner work,
I engender compassion for
myself and others.

TENETS

1. Inner work is a moment-to-moment, day-after-day, year-after-year, lifelong commitment and process.

2. When I genuinely do my inner work, denied parts of myself reveal themselves for purposes of integration and purification.

3. While engaging in my inner work, I invite my higher consciousness to aid me in the purification of my lower consciousness.

4. The fruits of my inner work are reflected in the quality of my inner state and manifest in the world through selfless service.

5. Inner work is psychological and spiritual in nature; meditation, contemplation, and self-inquiry facilitate my process.

6. I cannot have compassion for another without first having compassion for myself; consciously striving to have compassion for others strengthens having compassion for myself.

7. To be compassionate means to observe, but not identify with, the suffering of myself and others.

8. Compassion and truth are two major spiritual gifts I offer to those I serve.

With honesty and kindness,
I take responsibility for my own choices
and allow others to do the same.

TRIBUTE FIVE

TENETS

1. The courage to heal, grow and serve begins with being honest with myself about who I am and who I choose to become.

2. The well-being of myself and others depends on my ability to be honest without attack or condemnation.

3. Honesty asks that I speak the truth with compassion and self-responsibility.

4. I am free to choose my inner attitude regarding any given life circumstance; I can always choose again.

5. Once I choose again, I must do the inner work necessary to make that choice a reality.

6. I can only choose beliefs and attitudes for myself; I cannot choose them for another.

7. When I do not allow others to make their own choices or to take responsibility for themselves, I impose my will; by imposing my will, I disempower others, depriving them of the freedom of choice and the opportunity to discover their own uniqueness and their own inner strength.

8. I am responsible for the meaning and purpose I bring to my life and for choosing to learn and serve.

TRIBUTE SIX

I use each encounter as a reflection of either a remembrance of Divine Love or a grievance I continue to hold against myself or another.

TENETS

1. *All individuals are students and teachers to each other; in this way, there is meaning and purpose in every encounter.*

2. *What I see in others is a reflection of what I see in myself; what I see in myself, I project onto others.*

3. *When I react instead of respond, I am experiencing a denied part of myself; my reactions serve to remind me to continue my inner work.*

4. *Reflections of Divine Love come to me in many forms and serve as witnesses for my true reality, reminding me that I am not alone.*

5. *The extent to which I recognize and use reflections of Love or grievances as part of my inner work is dependent upon my willingness to be self-responsible.*

6. *The energy of my psyche is restricted by grievances I hold against myself, thereby limiting my creativity and service.*

7. *I can hold the space for resolution of a grievance for someone else only when I have released that same grievance within myself. Therefore, I hold the space for healing in others of that which has been healed within me.*

8. *All encounters involve service at some level and therefore have the potential for bringing comfort or for being a catalyst for change.*

I acknowledge the reciprocal relationship between giving and receiving, understanding that both are essential for the well-being of myself and others.

TRIBUTE SEVEN

TENETS

1. To receive and not to give results in an implosion of my energy, leading to narcissism and continued unmet needs.

2. To give while refusing to receive strengthens the arrogant belief that others are not worthy to give and that others, not I, need to receive.

3. I give to others by allowing myself to receive.

4. I am renewed and revitalized when I give selflessly; when I give, I am also being given to, I am receiving.

5. My experience of the outer world mirrors my inner beliefs concerning abundance and scarcity.

6. I am unconsciously giving and receiving all the time; the more conscious I am of the level on which I give and receive, the more helpful my giving and receiving is to the well-being of myself and others.

7. When I give, my energy moves outward and I manifest the fruits of my healing energy in the world.

8. Giving and receiving are human qualities that need nurturing and developing in early childhood and throughout life.

TRIBUTE EIGHT

I see the external reality of a situation as well as seeing beyond it to the personal lessons, inner strength, and spiritual essence of myself and others.

TENETS

1. *Serving others requires double vision, simultaneously seeing the facts of a circumstance and its deeper spiritual meaning.*

2. *Double vision develops through meditation, prayer, contemplation, self-inquiry, and inner work.*

3. *Discernment is an essential aspect of double vision; I develop discernment as I integrate psychological and spiritual knowledge with wisdom gained from life experiences.*

4. *When responding to a situation, I honor the self-responsibility of the choices of those involved while ensuring their physical and emotional safety.*

5. *I do not deny a person's behavior; I strive to see the inner spiritual strength present in the person although it may be temporarily inaccessible to them.*

6. *A spiritual essence is within all human beings; this essence is a manifestation of the spark of the Divine.*

7. *My responsibility in any situation is to remain focused on the condition of my inner state and my motivation for serving while simultaneously carrying out any action I am called to take.*

8. *My inner knowing determines how I respond in service in any situation.*

*I support my healing process and that of others
with patience, gentleness,
and unconditional acceptance.*

TRIBUTE
NINE

TENETS

1. *Support is having a loving manner.*

2. *The healing process unfolds in five stages: choosing to heal, making the commitment to do inner work, exploring alternatives, letting the process unfold, and acknowledging growth and healing.*

3. *Patience provides a psychological and spiritual space for healing to occur with greater integrity and depth.*

4. *The degree to which I release expectations of outcome in any given situation is the degree to which I am unconditionally accepting.*

5. *Unconditional acceptance sees the spiritual essence beyond an individual's behavior.*

6. *Gentleness provides a psychological and spiritual space that allows old patterns and beliefs to be disentangled and released.*

7. *The presence of patience, gentleness, and unconditional acceptance lessens resistance to change and growth.*

8. *When I genuinely support and honor my own healing process, I simultaneously honor and support that of others.*

TRIBUTE TEN

I accept the reality of the presence of Divine Love within my own mind and invite others to accept that same Love within themselves.

TENETS

1. Willingness to see differently results in recognizing that Divine Love resides in all minds.

2. Lack of self-love is the major obstacle to accepting the presence of Divine Love within myself.

3. Self-doubt keeps me from experiencing my true reality.

4. Accepting the presence of Divine Love within me is a prerequisite to accepting the presence of Divine Love in another.

5. Divine Love is reflected back to me from the loving mind of every person or living creature.

6. "To invite" is to provide a psychological and spiritual space in which persons feel emotionally safe to make new choices without fear of having my will imposed upon them.

7. In many ways and with different words, I practice inviting myself and others into the energy of Divine Love.

8. Naturally, with willingness and without effort, the energy expressed by my inner state extends to others my silent invitation to accept Divine Love. I have no expectations about when or if they will accept my offering.

SUPPORT FOR STAGE FIVE

Maintaining vigilance of one's personal will and its alignment with Divine Will is vital in this stage. It is strengthening to be in the company of others who have chosen to be on a spiritual path and to share mutual experiences, knowledge, and insight. Many find it helpful to explore metaphysics and mystical traditions within Eastern and Western religious thought. Transpersonal psychology offers the means to continue inner work.

The transition into Stage Six requires becoming fully anchored in a spiritual discipline that includes meditation, prayer, contemplation, self-inquiry, and direction from a spiritual teacher. From rigorous spiritual discipline, one acquires the quiet mind necessary to experience the purity of motivation and action that defines Selfless Action. One's actions reflect one's inner state at a deep spiritual level. In completing this shift from outer to inner focus, individuals become aware of the wealth of wisdom and spiritual guidance that resides within them.

An inner or outer spiritual teacher, who is a step ahead in understanding, assists in this awakening to inner knowledge. The choice of a spiritual teacher depends on each individual's preference for a tradition or school of thought. An outer teacher is one in physical form such as a guru, master, shaman, rabbi, priest, or other spiritually aware person. An inner teacher is one who appears or speaks in dreams, visions, or when one sits in silence. Such teachers might identify themselves as guides, as the Voice of God or Holy Spirit, or as a holy person such as Jesus, Mary, or Mohammed. At the right time, the need for a choice becomes apparent. One goes within and asks, waiting on inner guidance to point the way. The soul attracts that which best supports its evolution.

An outer teacher is one in physical form such as a guru, master, shaman, rabbi, priest, or other spiritually aware person. An inner teacher is one who appears or speaks in dreams, visions, or when one sits in silence.

A spiritual teacher also serves as a model for the appropriate use of the integration of feminine and masculine principles and demonstrates how to be a spiritual warrior on the physical plane.

A spiritual teacher can serve many purposes, some of which are: assistance in correcting errors in one's thought or belief system that affect one's life and service, support in living from a place of equanimity and true inner power, and help in learning how to come from right action and thus do selfless service.

A spiritual teacher also serves as a model for the appropriate use of the integration of feminine and masculine principles and demonstrates how to be a spiritual warrior on the physical plane. Such individuals are teachers of compassion and humility because they model patience and skill in communicating and relating to others with honor and respect.

Teachers provide an aura of energy that allows spiritual movement and evolution to take place. In this way, they show their students the next steps for growth and spiritual unfoldment. They demonstrate how to honor beauty, time, efficiency, and competence and thereby how to increase the availability of spiritual energy. A spiritual teacher can serve as a protector from negative forces and a guide during difficult and challenging times and at the time of death.

$\mathcal{S}$TAGE SIX

$\mathcal{S}$*elfless* $\mathcal{A}$*ction*

$\mathcal{B}$y 1982, a desire to experience the highest spiritual consciousness
began to blaze intensely within me. With certainty, I knew I wanted to be
free of fear, guilt, and discouragement and would do the necessary inner
work to bring this about.

I imagined there to be an actual inner state that ceaselessly radiated an
energy field of purity and clarity, upliftment, and right action. I pondered
how one acquired and maintained an unbroken connection with the source of
such a high state. Whether called the Transpersonal Self, Christ Consciousness, Buddha Mind, Guru Principle, God, or Goddess, I knew this was the
Force I wanted to have direct my life, my actions, and my service. I desperately wanted this Force to work through me.

I began to study the lives of saints, renowned and obscure, who had expressed their service while being in this uplifted state. In every person I met,
I sought to recognize this level of consciousness. Was it possible to see the
Presence everywhere and to see Its energy working through others? Was it
possible for Its energy to work through me, most, if not all, of the time? Was

this what was meant by inner freedom and true joy? I wondered.

With the help of a spiritual teacher, I recognized that the potential of experiencing this pure, God-centered inner state resides within all of us. Living with an attitude of selfless service is the reflection of this state and the ultimate purpose of our respective spiritual journeys. We are born to learn how to serve the Inner Self, the God-Self within ourselves and others, and in this way to live in the consciousness of the True Self.

DESCRIPTION:
SELFLESS ACTION

In Stage Six, people live in the awareness that a force greater than themselves is the true doer and that they are the instruments through which this force expresses itself. They become spontaneous and ceaseless radiations of the True Self, fully accepting their purpose, mission, and destiny. They live and serve with precision, respect, presence, and right action. Unattached to the fruits of action, the uniqueness of the personality becomes a conduit of expression of the True Self. Because they spontaneously radiate divine energy, the aura of their presence is healing.

Entry into this stage necessitates purification and relinquishment of any remaining selfish and hidden motivations for service. In this stage, such motivations no longer exist. The individual has assimilated the nutrients from the learnings of multiple life experiences and allowed the outer shell hiding and defending the true identity to fall away. The individual is now ready and prepared to experience an unobstructed and unending flow of divine energy.

Throughout life to this point, serving others has functioned as a purifying agent for the ego's defensiveness. True Service is not tainted with ego needs. Selfless action arises from union with the Absolute; the server is totally open to a divine view of serving the world. Every action is a prayer, a service to the True Self within oneself and others, and an acknowledgment of love for humanity. In this way, service is the altar of devotion.

Some time ago I had a dream that taught how True Service expresses as devotion to others.

A saint from India visited my hometown of Kouts, Indiana. To prepare for her arrival, the town rented the

STATEMENT:
Service is the altar of devotion.

CORE LEARNING:
Being service

SALIENT FEAR:
I remember fear, but I am fearless.

PRIMARY GIFT:
Steady Wisdom

TRANSITIONAL SHIFT:
Surrender of the physical body for service in a higher realm

one-hundred-year-old school house that had been re-modeled as an apartment building in 1950. The saint treated the building as a school, bringing all of her help-ers with the intention of staying a long time. She and her helpers put on an elaborate conference covering many topics about how to attain spiritual well-being.

Every action is a prayer, a service to the Self within oneself and others, and an acknowledgment of love for humanity. In this way, service is the altar of devotion.

I was worried about how an Indian saint would be received in this small Midwestern farming community. With relief, I observed that people attending the confer-ence began to have spiritual transformations. I won-dered how she knew that Kouts was my hometown since I had not told her. I sensed that she cared deeply about the well-being of Kouts and honored its residents. I knew I cared deeply about them as well and have always been very grateful for the valuable learning I received from my life there.

In the dream, the saint represented a state of consciousness that related to others as though they were her devotional altar. She offered, without intrusion and imposition, the right kind of service at the right time in the right amount for the right rea-son. The location of the conference was in a building that sym-bolized the learning of past generations. She was willing to pro-vide the expertise and time needed to provide a new level of spiritual understanding. Her capable helpers who joined her vision assisted her. She was a prototype of service who knew how to provide a proper setting to allow for spiritual transforma-tion. She was willing to do this even for those "hidden away" in a small country town in the Midwest who were seemingly un-aware of her. I asked myself: Was it my love and gratitude for my childhood home that had drawn a saint to this place? Did love attract the purity of a saint's service? Is the saint's devotion to service her expression of Divine Love?

The Divine Love that resides within each of us invites us to use our life experiences for the purpose of awakening the innate knowledge of the soul. When we intentionally use our life experiences as opportunities for spiritual learning, our thoughts and motivations are purified and the soul's knowledge emerges. Sometimes, Divine Love penetrates our being so deeply that It purifies deep and unconscious tendencies that have impeded our spiritual growth, perhaps for lifetimes.

I was taught about Stage Six through one of the most profound purification experiences guided by Divine Love that I have personally experienced. It occurred some years ago when I had to make a difficult decision in my workplace. I call this episode my "Arjuna Initiation" because I felt like the warrior prince, Arjuna, in the *Bhagavad Gita*, a sacred text from India.

Arjuna is overcome by the horrors of war and refuses to engage in battle. The divine Krishna, acting as his charioteer, teaches him that life is a battle and that he must do what needs to be done. Krishna exhorts Arjuna to enter the battle of life fully, despite its horrendous obstacles and challenges, and to move always and resolutely forward.

Like Arjuna, I had to learn how to do what needed to be done by concentrating on action and not on the fruits of action. Like Arjuna, I had to surrender my actions to the Unknowable Absolute and not shrink from my duty and responsibility. I had to face my own shadow and its unconscious motives and hidden impurities. Like Arjuna, I had to decide whether I was living my life for personal gain or as an instrument of Divine Will.

As can often occur when one is ready for a major purification of unconscious motives and a subsequent shift in spiritual

When we intentionally use our life experiences as opportunities for spiritual learning, our thoughts and motivations are purified and the soul's knowledge emerges.

consciousness, other people and those in unseen realms provide help and support. In this case, I was alerted to the forthcoming event through a dream.

By continually seeking for and becoming dependent upon the approval of others, I eventually lost the awareness of my own truth and, therefore, my own dharma.

    I stood before an altar at the beginning of a cave. Helpers were nearby who explained that I had to take a dangerous and life-threatening journey deep into the earth. Two women were assigned to go with me to ensure that my journey would be a safe and successful one. They had each successfully taken the journey and, therefore, knew when to alert me to danger and when to rescue me. I bowed with reverence before the holy altar and, with my two protectors, began the journey into the dark underground. Many times I fell into an abyss and became lost in the darkness; each time, the women pulled me to safety and guided me to the next challenge.

    I eventually reached safety on the other side of the cave. Although I experienced tremendous gratitude for the devoted and competent service of the two women, I knew that the True Self within me had provided the spiritual strength I needed to pass this spiritual test.

Within two months of this dream, I began my Arjuna Initiation. My *dharma* or work in the world has been to provide leadership in helping professions, specifically to nonprofit and private service and teaching organizations. Throughout my life, however, I had felt simultaneously inspired and ambivalent about being a leader, and I had never resolved this issue. As a result I carried many Stage Four co-dependency issues into Stage Five.

By continually seeking for and becoming dependent upon the approval of others, I eventually lost the awareness of my own truth and, therefore, my own *dharma*. My inner self-forgetting led to co-dependent relationships with inappropriate communication boundaries. I could not say no. I denied the existence of conflict and differences. I did not discern who was and was not a safe person to tell my most inner thoughts and would subsequently feel betrayed. I often played the willing helper role by endlessly listening to the interpersonal problems of others rather than encouraging them to work out their issues among themselves. I took on the responsibility for the well-being of others.

My inner ambivalence had greatly affected the organization I led, resulting in confusion among members about the purpose of our work and the intent of my actions. The organization became a ship with a crew but no captain. When others tried to take on the captain role, authority conflicts arose and accusations prevailed. No longer feeling safe, I, as leader, became emotionally and mentally vulnerable. I thought I was going to die from the stress of the tremendous ambivalence within my psyche and the subsequent loss of mental, emotional, and physical energy.

Like Arjuna, I was helped by those more advanced than I. Stage Six teachers supported me while I gradually came to learn, grow, and heal from the consequences of abdicating my *dharma*. Like Arjuna, I had been tempted to not do my duty. Fortunately, also like Arjuna, I finally surrendered to Divine Will and the power of the Absolute. Without the presence and help of these Stage Six individuals who walked through the initiation with me and provided devotional service, however, I know I would not be alive today.

Through my own intimate and very real life experience, I respect those who abide in the pure inner state of devotional service. Having personally received the spiritual gifts of such sacred service, I welcome the time when I am ready to move into the exquisite state of Stage Six.

Without the presence and help of these Stage Six individuals who walked through the initiation with me and provided devotional service, however, I know I would not be alive today.

PROCESS OF SELFLESS ACTION

STATE OF THE SELF

Mystics value the ordinary; "insignificance" is what matters and not fantasies of power and fame.

Individuals enter the stage of selfless action once they totally surrender to the Eternal *Dharma* of right living and to their *dharma* or duty in the world. This surrender is conscious and occurs at an inner level. They are now fully aware that the Absolute is the Source and that their inner divinity is the true reality. From this place, they are at one with Divine Will and honor all sentient beings. They are mystics.

Mystics have developed and integrated all conscious and unconscious aspects of the human psyche. The personal will and its energy, skill, and goodness are a reflection of the Transpersonal Will. The personal self no longer feels separated from the True Self. They recognize that as spontaneous radiations of the Absolute living in the world, they can, with others' willingness, effect changes deep within other individuals. Mystics value the ordinary; "insignificance" is what matters and not fantasies of power and fame.

WORLD VIEW

The world view of Stage Six is one of nonduality, of both/and, which sees the potential of learning and growth within all circumstances. True happiness is not sought outside but allowed to emerge from within. Mystics have been purified and have submitted to rigorous teaching by authentic spiritual teachers, both seen and unseen.

Mystics live life fully by seeking to do what needs to be done in the moment. They focus on actions, not on expectations or the fruits of the action. They know that by focusing with one-pointedness on the means to inner peace, they automatically achieve that goal.

RELATIONSHIP WITH GOD

Self-effort and Divine Grace allow mystics to surrender into the awareness of the Unknowable Absolute, into a state of complete safety and comfort in not knowing. This is the state of emptiness, that state of One in which nothing material clings, that state in which only Consciousness exists. Guidance and protection from the higher realms support safe transition into the finer vibrations of this stage.

To claim ownership of true spiritual knowledge, mystics bring this wisdom into the world and ground it in the practical tasks of daily life. They focus attention in the present moment, the now in which the True Self exists. Mystics trust that the divine energy permeates all action and being. They work with precision, knowing that the Absolute is in the details.

PREDOMINATE SHADOW ISSUES

Persons in this stage have moved out of darkness, yet do not forget nor fail to recognize the nature and qualities of darkness. They understand that the more enlightened they become, the more vigilant they must be about their shadow side. They maintain this vigilance by acknowledging the nature of duality while standing in the place of creative synthesis. With this understanding, they become able guides and helpers to those who wish to move out of duality into a full and complete awareness of the One.

The temptation to return to duality is ever-present, yet is counterbalanced by the strength of the Absolute. A fall from grace or regression to a lower stage of spiritual development becomes possible if there is any failure to maintain vigilance or failure to maintain the spiritual disciplines upon which one's level of spiritual vibration depends.

To claim ownership of true spiritual knowledge, mystics bring this wisdom into the world and ground it in the practical tasks of daily life.

Regression is also possible if they have not fully experienced and integrated all the lessons of their lives. Partial understandings can convince them that they are at a level of spiritual realization actually not reached. Denying one's weakness and priding oneself on one's spiritual attainments leads to relaxed vigilance and subsequent succumbing to the pull of sex, power, and money. These aspects of life must be fully understood and clear life choices made to avert the danger of this kind of regression.

This highest and greatest level of giving reflects an unwavering, sustained commitment to God and all sentient beings.

MODE OF SERVICE

Because those in Stage Six have evolved to a state of selfless action, they exemplify the highest levels of service as **duty**, **charity**, **purification**, and **devotion**. They now live selflessly on behalf of the spiritual well-being and growth of others. Maimonides wrote that service is selfless when a person gives without knowing to whom the gift is made and the recipient does not know from whom he receives. This highest and greatest level of giving reflects an unwavering, sustained commitment to God and all sentient beings.

To remain established in an inner state that expresses selfless action, one must know how to live and care for one's human life in such a way that one can:

- maintain the quality and strength of divine energy,

- maintain an uncompromised discipline of spiritual practice,

- maintain focus on personal *dharma* and on Eternal *Dharma*,

- be securely anchored in receiving support and guidance from the Inner Voice,

- be knowledgeable of spiritual scripture and live spiritual teachings with integrity, and

- live a life based on spiritual rather than ego-based principles.

Achieving mastery in this stage necessitates a profound understanding of the universal principle that giving and receiving are the same. Because the ego is no longer defended against the energy of Divine Love, the inner spiritual vessel is continuously full and ever increasing in power and purity. Like an endless river of spiritual nectar, the more divine energy flows out, the more flows in; the more that flows in, the more flows out.

In this stage of the evolution of service, the individual has the unique ability to control how much energy flows and where it flows. In this way, divine energy, directed by Divine Will, emanates from the individual in a manner that serves the highest good of others. The mystic accurately perceives and reads the energy fields of others, seeing what obstacles to spiritual progress reside in the subtle body. He or she can instantaneously become aware of what is needed to remove these obstacles and what the person is ready to learn and needs to learn to make spiritual progress.

The universal principles that guided the Healing the Healer stage now shift from a dualistic choice of perception to one established in the absolute certainty of Oneness. One *is* divine. One *is* an instrument of Divine Will. One *is* devotional service.

The mystic accurately perceives and reads the energy fields of others, seeing what obstacles to spiritual progress reside in the subtle body.

THE UNIVERSAL TRIBUTES FOR MASTERY

1. *My will is an instrument of Divine Will.*

2. *I serve with joy, spontaneity, and gratitude.*

3. *I have no expectations or attachment to the form of my service or to the fruits of my actions.*

4. *I have compassion for all sentient beings.*

5.   *I allow others to make choices using their will.*

6.   *I ceaselessly remember God's Love in all interactions.*

7.   *I experience giving and receiving as the same.*

8.   *I see beyond appearances to the Divine Love in others.*

9.   *I serve with patience, gentleness, and unconditionality.*

10.   *I am a reflection of God's Love.*

The universal principles that guided the Healing the Healer stage now shift from a dualistic choice of perception to one established in the absolute certainty of Oneness. One is divine. One is an instrument of Divine Will. One is devotional service.

Descriptions of spiritual development leading to selfless service are found in both Eastern and Western religious traditions. In Buddhism, for example, individuals who are in the stage of selfless action are called *Bodhisattvas*. *Bodhisattvas* serve at the level of the cause of suffering, which Buddhism defines as attachment to desires in the material world. *Bodhisattvas* serve society while in a state of joy, humility, equanimity, patience, perseverance, unshakable confidence, oneness, and silence.

In Christianity, people in the third or unitive stage of spiritual development experience total peace and stillness and serve others by their presence of purity, humility, and innocence. In this stage, there is no psychological conflict, no interference with duty, and no lack of understanding of others. They have pure hearts and have great control and mastery over their behavior with little or no effort. They no longer have ego defenses. To them the presence of Christ is everywhere. The mind and will are open to God; there are no obstacles. They only experience and express gifts of the Holy Spirit.

In the sacred traditions of India, *seva* or devotional service to God is the most highly evolved expression of service. To serve selflessly is to love God and love one's neighbor more than oneself. True service is knowing intuitively what is needed or not needed and is done out of joy, not out of obligation nor for payment. Like Arjuna, they dedicate all action to divinity; they act not for self but for God.

The *Dharma Shastra* scriptures describe the life of the renunciate. Renunciation at the inner level involves cultivating discipline and offering one's life to the highest. Inner renunciation results in letting go of all attachments to possessions, places, and people. Those in this stage of life may choose to live solitary lives or to serve in a multitude of roles, most visibly as teachers. A renunciate is an inspiring reminder of a life dedicated to God.

Once the first six stages are mastered, one still lives a life of spiritual unfoldment and service, yet from a different perspective. Past, present, and future are all one. At the time of death, one is fully conscious.

> *The spiritual mountain must be climbed step by step.*
> *It is a journey made alone, though it need not be lonely.*
> *We walk with others awhile, we pass and are passed.*
> *We meet teachers and stop to learn;*
>   *we meet students and stop to teach.*
> *We slide into an abyss and are pulled out*
>   *to help someone else from a dark cave.*
> *We must walk each step of the path, avoiding none.*
> *We must resolve any obstacles we find in the way;*
>   *there are no detours, although we are free to turn back.*
> *By moving forward, facing and conquering obstacles,*
>   *we acquire the tremendous inner strength and wisdom to*
>   *walk on.*
> *We anchor strength in the Unknowable Absolute,*
>   *secure in the knowledge of the True Self.*
>
> *We become the mountain.*

True service is knowing intuitively what is needed or not needed and is done out of joy, not out of obligation nor for payment.

STAGE SEVEN

Beyond the Physical

One afternoon in late 1974, after years of severe depression and inner distress, I knelt down and with all my heart begged God for help. A week later, I spontaneously drew an intricately detailed geographical map. Synchronistically, while I drew the map, a friend received inner messages for me from "The Guides" about a previous life that closely paralleled events and people in my present life. We were told that the map was of the world in 200 A.D.

For the next five years, The Guides served both of us as inner counselors and teachers, leading us through steps and stages of inner healing. At no time did The Guides impose their will on us. From this most personal and intensely healing experience, I "knew" the strength and resources I needed were indeed within me and that help could come from unseen realms.

DESCRIPTION:
BEYOND THE PHYSICAL

For the past three decades there has been a steady increase in books and research about near death experiences and a proliferation of people who "channel" entities from "the other side." Information about physical death and the experience of dying has also become common place. From around the world come reports of apparitions of and phenomena related to the Virgin Mary, Jesus, and numerous saints.

None of this is new. In India in centuries past and to the present day, saintly teachers dematerialize or are seen in physical form in more than one place at the same time. Both ancient and advanced cultures like the Greeks, and indigenous cultures, like the Australian aboriginal and Native American tribes, consulted oracles and relied on seers who were connected to other worldly guidance. In the Victorian era, seances and spiritualism gained popularity. During World War II, Father Padre Pio, a priest in a village in Italy, appeared in a cloud to American fighter pilots, causing them to turn back from their mission; he was also seen ministering to the wounded on a battlefield far from the village he had never left. The signs and phenomena accompanying the apparitions of the Virgin Mary at Lourdes, Fatima, and Medjugorje have been witnessed by millions. Media technology is now able to acquaint people, accurately or not, with the plethora of information regarding evidence of the nonphysical realm. As with any popularized trend, charlatans, myths, and rumors abound. Beneath all of this, however, is a seed of truth.

The seventh stage of service, Beyond the Physical, acknowledges the existence of life after death and proposes that the soul continues its life and its evolution of service after leaving the physical body. This stage acknowledges helpers not in physical form

The seventh stage of service, Beyond the Physical, acknowledges the existence of life after death and proposes that the soul continues its life and its evolution of service after leaving the physical body.

and the potential each of us has of becoming one of these helpers after death.

Various realms where souls reside are described in a number of sacred texts, such as the *Bible,* the *Kabbalah,* the *Koran,* the *Shiva Sutras,* the *Tibetan Book of the Dead,* the *Upanishads,* and the *Vedas.*

Determining the authenticity of help from the unseen realms, such as from inner teachers, guides, or angelic beings, is a personal and necessary task. No one can tell us what is right for us or who and what we should listen to. Ken Carey who wrote *The Starseed Transmission* once commented in a speech that just because a soul is two thousand years old is no reason to assume it is any wiser than you are.

There are two major criteria to use in establishing the authenticity of unseen helpers. First, authentic beings from the unseen realms offer support and protection that does not impose itself upon our own integrity and choices. They offer help by sending or suggesting thoughts and ideas. They make it clear, however, that we are to check these thoughts and ideas with our own sense of inner rightness. Help from beyond is offered with an attitude of invitation and consideration. We are free to accept or reject the help.

Second, unseen helpers never suggest psychological, physical, or spiritual harm to ourselves or others. Blame, justification, and victimization are discouraged and emphasis is placed on compassion, right action, and true understanding. Often, helpers provide a universal philosophical context in which to view our experiences of life on earth.

Individuals in each of the six stages of awareness differ in how they view and use help that comes from beyond the physical plane. Those in the first stage, Awakening to Serve, are often open to

Individuals in each of the six stages of awareness differ in how they view and use help that comes from beyond the physical plane.

these realms. Because they have not yet established a sense of self, however, they have difficulty assessing the authenticity of their experience. They also tend to give their personal power away to what appears to be a higher authority, believing this authority knows what's best for them. Those in Stage Two, the Work Ethic, and Stage Three, the Missionary Attitude, typically discount the existence of these realms or define them in a rigid way, depending upon their religious or lack of religious orientation.

Wounded Healers in Stage Four deepen their interest and knowledge in matters beyond the physical plane, yet, like Stage One, they are vulnerable to giving their personal power away to a seemingly higher and outer authority. Wounded Healers may or may not use this knowledge with pride when helping others. Stage Five, Healing the Healer, commonly experiences a close connection beyond the physical plane and can use this gift either as a source of wisdom or as a source of power over others. Stage Six, Selfless Action, is knowledgeable about the breadth of these realms and communicates with them while remaining fully conscious of participating in the world.

Help from beyond the physical can be offered to anyone at any time in any stage. One does not have to be in an advanced stage of service to receive this offering. Individuals are equally respected, valued, and honored by the helpers who follow the Will of the Absolute. An attitude saying, "Look at me! I must be extra special, and certainly more special than you, to have these wonderful and other-worldly experiences," reflects a shadow that disowns its gold. Always, behind pride and competitiveness, lies unacknowledged strength and hidden potential.

One does not have to be in an advanced stage of service to receive this offering.

Help from the seeming beyond informs and comforts you.
You are not alone.

PART THREE

Unveiling
the Soul

…as we grow clear and open,

the more complete the joy of heaven is.

–Dante Alighieri

$\mathcal{I}$NTRODUCTION

$\mathcal{A}$ spiritual warrior represents the part of us that is willing to confront emotional pain and has the fortitude and stamina to persist in the healing process even if it takes many years.

In becoming a spiritual warrior, an understanding of the nature of the psyche is extremely important. The psyche can be imaged as a house with different levels and rooms. The ground floor represents the conscious self, the upper floors the higher self, and the basement the lower self. During our waking hours we relate to others and are nurtured on the ground floor, represented by the living room and kitchen. The basement is used for storage for those things we rarely use, things we want to keep for future needs, or things we have no further use for but do not want to throw away. The upstairs represents the higher self, a place where we store prized belongings and where we dream our highest dreams. There are closets throughout the house where additional items of various sorts are stored. What is visible in a house may be relatively little compared to what is put away.

So it is with our psyches. We have a conscious self, a personality, through which we operate in daily life. We have a subconscious, or shadow, in which many aspects and memories are put away, some very hidden and forgotten for years and some no longer useful but to which we still cling. We also have a higher self, the True Self, which remembers its identity with the Absolute and which longs to express itself in the world through our personality.

Inner work, the work of exploring and healing the psyche, requires the stance of the warrior. From this strong and steadfast place within us, we can move through the healing process, cleaning, sorting, esteeming, accepting, until we know and integrate all parts of ourselves.

STRUCTURE OF PART THREE

This section of the book is a guide for you as individuals or groups to use in understanding the role service plays in your lives and in exploring hidden motivations for serving.

You are the sculptor of your soul and of your life. The in-depth study suggested here is one way to use your life circumstances for the inner work that will reveal the unique masterpiece of your soul. The daily giving and receiving in work, relationships, and solitude comprise service. We are all servers, and we are being served all the time, even in our dreams and especially in our prayers. Together we sculpt the collective souls of our families, businesses, organizations, countries, and world.

In five sections, Part Three presents ways in which you can learn to use service as a tool for the inner work of sculpting your soul. The Process Of Study consists of suggestions for studying the book, practicing the Universal Tributes, and supplemental reading. The other four sections consist of questionnaires and exercises related to the shadow of service. Through them you can survey your attitudes and motivations, learn centering methods in preparation for working with the shadow, and identify and explore your shadow of service.

Before he began each piece of sculpture, Michelangelo spent months in preparation. He studied each subject intensively, reviewing related art and literature. Only then did he begin to make sketches and visual studies for his work. Sometimes to meet the criteria of his patron or to achieve the desired effect, he had to acquire new skills, find new tools, and learn new techniques. He communed with the marble, learning its nature and discovering its soul. Finally, when he took hammer to chisel, he never struck a wrong blow.

Each of us has within us the potential for crafting our inner being with the skill, commitment, and devotion of a Michelangelo. Each of us can choose to dedicate our lives to the preparation and study necessary to unveil service as the masterpiece of the soul that awaits within us.

Study Guide

*T*he great Tibetan saint Milarepa was meditating one day when three bellicose demons appeared at the mouth of his cave. Rattling skulls and bloody swords, shrieking obscenities, and exuding the smell of rotting flesh, they entered the cave howling like a hurricane. With a great smile and a grand gesture, he bid them sit by the fire and "take tea."

"But aren't you terrified by our appearance?!" the demons demanded. "Not at all," whispered Milarepa, adding something like: "It is at moments like this, when the demons of fear and doubt present themselves, that I am most grateful to be on the path of healing, to be a yogi. Come, take tea. Make yourself comfortable. You are always welcome. Your hideous visage only reminds me to be aware and have mercy. Come take tea!" [1]

---

[1] Stephen Levine, *Healing Into Life and Death*. (New York: Doubleday, 1987) p. 222.

PROCESS OF STUDY

The intent of this study guide is to support the integrity of your unique way of being and serving in the world. I recommend these steps prior to proceeding with your study:

- Return to each of the stages of awareness and contemplate your life experiences as they relate to the characteristics within each of the stages. Note which stage best describes your present experience of service, identifying what you feel is your current motivation for service.

- Select a personal quality that you would like to develop and express in your life and thus in your service.

- Contemplate the level of your commitment to purifying your motivation for service.

- Acknowledge your steps in growth and awareness about service.

You can decide to use this material with varying degrees of involvement:

- Read quickly through the material to gain an overview of its contents and return it when ready to do deeper work.

- Focus on removing the obstacles to the awareness of True Service by working with the exercises for resolving shadow and misapplication tendencies that affect service.

- Select only those exercises which serve your needs.

- Along with or separate from doing the exercises, commit to studying the Universal Tributes and their tenets. Choose one Tribute per day or one per week. Read it and its tenets in the morning and again in the evening.

The mystic, endowed with native talents... and following... the instruction of a master, enters the waters and finds he can swim....

—JOSEPH CAMPBELL

*"I do this.
I do that."
The big black
snake of
selfishness has
bitten you!*

*"I do nothing."
This is the nectar
of faith,
So drink and be
happy!*

—THE
ASHTAVAKRA GITA

Recall the tribute several times during the day. After the evening reading, contemplate any insights that have arisen during the day and write them in a journal. Once you have completed the ten Tributes, begin again. Make a long-term commitment to this study.

- Journaling will assist you in observing the process and progress of your awareness of service. You may want to keep a log of your insights and awarenesses, adding various drawings, affirmations, saying or pictures which reinforce your learning process about service.

This study guide can be used by individuals, groups, and organizations who wish to develop a deeper understanding of what it means to serve and to be a server.

Joining with a friend or study group can be particularly useful and supportive. Two people can serve as "server partners" for one another, facilitating and supporting each other's process. Partners can share their responses to the self-inquiry questions and their experiences with the various exercises. Study group members might take turn facilitating a given chapter, topic, or stage.

Both for-profit and nonprofit organizations may find the study guide material instructive in understanding the role of motivation in service and how motivation affects the quality of service. Establishing study and support groups for servers might be appropriate in work settings ready to expand their awareness and quality of service.

For optimal use of this material, individuals and organizations need to be open to acknowledging unrealized potential and recognizing projection, denial, and neglect in service. When you know that a reservoir of creativity and psychological and spiritual strength lies hidden within you, you can safely commit to working with your shadow and thus to improving the quality of your service.

The dynamic relationship between your service and your shadow is true whether your service is visible in your career, place of employment, in your volunteer work, family, or social interactions. The ultimate goal of shadow work in service is to help you to become yourself and to birth your unique being into the world. Shadow work helps you develop your full potential and live your unique life.

The purpose of this workbook is threefold. It provides ways for connecting with the inner strength needed to do shadow work, methods for identifying shadow tendencies when in service and psychological tools for working with hidden motivations for service.

The following four books are recommended as supplementary reading to this workbook: Robert Johnson's *Owning Your Own Shadow*, Connie Zweig and Jeremiah Abrams' *Meeting the Shadow*, Charles Whitfield's *Boundaries and Relationships*, and Piero Ferrucci's *What We May Be*. These authors provide the reader with an understanding of the nature of the human psyche and its shadow.

Be sensitive to your emotional state as you work with the exercises and suggestions in this workbook. Healing as a natural process takes time. If at any time you feel overwhelmed or confused set the material aside. Immediately tend to your psychological well-being by doing one or more of the following: read uplifting or inspiring books or articles, listen to soothing music, contemplate on uplifting qualities, meditate, or go for a walk in nature.

The ultimate goal of shadow work in service is to help you to become yourself and to birth your unique being into the world.

SURVEYING ATTITUDES AND MOTIVATIONS ABOUT SERVICE

Most people have not taken the time for an in-depth exploration of their motivations and intentions about service. If this is true for you, you may find it helpful to evaluate your present attitudes and motivations about service. It is important to explore your motivations *before* beginning any work with your shadow.

Service Questionnaire

Contemplate and respond to the following questions. Thoroughly answer them and avoid statements of generalities and platitudes. You may want to periodically return to these questions and respond to them with greater clarity and honesty.

1. What are my beliefs about serving (helping) others?

2. Am I aware that I help others in my life? In what ways do I feel I help others?

3. What are my beliefs about being helped by others?

4. Am I aware that I have received help in my life? In what ways do I feel I have been helped?

5. How does helping (giving) relate to being helped (receiving)?

6. How would I describe my own shadow of service, i.e. what attitudes, prejudices, or behaviors do I have that adversely affect the quality of my service?

7. Do I feel I have a specific calling, a mission in my life? What is this calling and when was I first aware of it?

8. What impact, if any, did the church or my spiritual tradition have on me regarding my desire to help others?

9. How does "making a living" to meet my and/or my family's financial needs relate to my helping others?

10. How does being of service relate to my emotional well-being?

One can give nothing whatever without giving oneself—
that is to say, risking oneself. If one cannot risk oneself, then one is simply incapable of giving.

–JAMES BALDWIN

11. How does being of service relate to my spirituality?

12. Who have been models for me regarding how to serve (help) others and why have they been so?

The following exercises help identify how your life experiences relate to the nature and quality of your service.

Laws of Service Exercise

Expand your awareness of the laws of service by applying them to specific events in your life in which you either gave or received service. Chapter One gives an example for working with the laws in this way.

Life Inventory Exercise

Explore the role service has played in your life by taking a personal inventory. Draw lines to form three columns on a page. In the first column, identify a significant event in your life. Describe the feelings you experienced about this event in a second column. In the third column, describe what service you offer to others that reflects the wisdom you have gleaned from this event. For example, you might have failed a test in school, which resulted in feelings of low self-worth and isolation. Your gift of service might be as an example of one who understands that failure has the potential of redirecting and strengthening one's life.

PREPARING TO WORK WITH THE SHADOW

Centering and witnessing are prerequisite practices to doing shadow work. These practices expand our psychological space and enable us to connect with our inner strength. Remember to always center

*All that matters
is to be at one
with the
living God,
to be a creature
in the house
of the
God of Life.*

–D. H. LAWRENCE

yourself and engage your Witness Self *before* and *during* any shadow work.

You are centered when you focus your attention on the belly, the neutral center of gravity of your body. Your belly safely contains your physical, psychological, and spiritual energies. You experience a sense of psychological spaciousness and stability when you bring your attention to the center of your body. Practice centering and witnessing exercises *daily* so they become second nature to you. You will find it comforting to center and witness at any time and in any situation in which you feel anxious, fearful, angry, or confused.

Remember to always center yourself and engage your Witness Self before and during any shadow work.

Centering Exercise [2]

Sit in a relaxed position with your feet flat on the floor. Gently close your eyes.

Breathe slowly and consciously. Breathe in, breathe out; breathe in, breathe out. Allow the body to breathe all by itself.

Now, take a deep relaxing breath and breathe out any tension in the body.

Breathe in, bringing energy up from the earth into your feet, legs, and body. Breathe out, bringing the energy down through your feet into the earth. Allow yourself to feel firmly planted on the earth.

Gently inhale, bringing the energy up from the earth, filling and refreshing the body. Exhale, releasing into the earth any thoughts or feelings you may be experiencing.

Breathe in, allowing energy to flow through the body; breathe out, dropping your attention to your belly, your center of gravity, about two inches below your navel.

---

[2] Written by Karen Watt.

Now continue to breathe in and out in your own natural rhythm with your attention focused in your belly.

If any feelings or thoughts come up, breathe them down into the earth and return your focus of attention to the belly.

Allow the belly to steady yourself.

Allow yourself to fully experience the center of yourself.

Holding your attention in the belly, gently open your eyes.

Witnessing Exercise:
Disidentification and Self-identification [3]

Sit in a comfortable and relaxed position. Slowly take a few deep breaths and center yourself. Then make the following affirmations, slowly and thoughtfully:

I have a body, but I am not my body. I am more than that.
My body may be in different conditions of health or sickness. It may be rested or tired, but it is not my real "I."
My body is my precious instrument of experience and of action, but it is not my self.
I have a body, but I am not my body.
I am the one who is aware.

I have emotions, but I am more than my emotions.
My emotions are countless, contradictory, changing.
Yet, I know that I always remain I, my self, in a state of
  irritation or calm.

Since I can observe, understand, and judge my emotions,
And then increasingly dominate, direct, and utilize them,
it is evident that they are not my self.
I have emotions, but I am not my emotions.
I am more than that.
I am the one who is aware.

Remember: the 4 causes of suffering – not getting what you want –getting what you want and not being satisfied with it –being separated from those or that which you love –having to endure the company of those or that which you do not love.

—CHERI HUBER

[3] Adapted from Roberto Assagioli, *The Act of Will*, pp. 214-215.

I have an intellect, but I am more than my intellect.
My intellect may be quiet or active.
It is capable of expanding, letting go of limiting beliefs, and
learning new attitudes.
It is an organ of knowledge in regard to the inner world as
well as the outer.
But it is not my self.
I have an intellect, but I am not my intellect.
I am more than that.
I am the one who is aware.

I am a center of pure self-awareness.
I am a center of will,
Capable of mastering and directing all my energies:
physical, emotional, mental, and spiritual.
I am the one who is aware.
I am the self.

As you use this process, you may want to change it to serve
your own situation or your own feelings. For example, if you have
issues with your job, you could design an "I have a job, but I am
not my job" statement fitting your job issues. If you have intense
feelings of anger about someone, you could affirm, "I have anger,
but I am not my anger."

IDENTIFYING THE SHADOW OF SERVICE

Service is an integral part of every activity of our lives. As
such, our shadow of service can potentially reveal itself in any
interaction we have with another. Interactions might be with
family, friends, colleagues, or people we meet in passing. They
might occur in settings such as a school, workplace, organization,
neighborhood store, or government agency. There is no end to
the settings in which potentially we either give or receive service.

The more a man learns whole-heartedly to confront the world which threatens him with isolation, the more are the depths of the Ground of Being revealed and the possibilities of new life and Becoming opened.

—KARLFRIED GRAF
VON DÜRKHEIM

Therefore, we have endless opportunities to integrate our shadow energy and to learn and grow.

The following methods can help you identify the tendencies of your shadow that are impacting the quality of your service.

SELF-INQUIRY

Asking self-inquiry questions *during or after you have given or received service* helps identify and monitor your motivations for service. All self-inquiry questions are variations of "Why am I doing this?" and "Who does this really serve." The following are examples of self-inquiry questions. You may also want to create questions of your own.

Self-Inquiry Questionnaire

1. What qualities or attributes am I trying to hide from those I serve?

2. Of what am I accusing those I serve? Can I acknowledge that those qualities or attributes are also within myself?

3. Is my action contributing in any way to my own, others', or the world's misery?

4. Am I acknowledging the capabilities and strengths of the person I am serving?

5. Am I expecting a specific outcome or result of my service?

6. Am I seeing the gifts and talents of others but not my own?

7. Am I willing to give but not to receive?

8. Am I viewing my emotional reactions as learning and healing opportunities?

And the truth is that as a man's real power grows and his knowledge widens, ever the way he can follow grows narrower: until at last he chooses nothing, but does only and wholly what he must do.

–URSULA K. LEGUIN

Only in silence and solitude, in the quiet of worship, the reverent peace of prayer, the adoration in which the entire ego-self silences and abases itself in the presence of the Invisible God to receive His one Word of Love; only in these "activities" which are "non-actions" does the spirit truly wake from the dream of a multifarious, confused, and agitated existence.

—THOMAS MERTON

9. Do I feel that those I serve take my energy and emotional health away from me?

10. Do I take responsibility for the choices, feelings, and actions of those I serve?

11. Am I fearful, doubtful, or judgemental about the people I serve or myself?

12. Am I impatient with those I serve or with myself?

13. Do I desire recognition, awards, or constant appreciation for my service?

14. Do I believe one form of service is superior to another?

15. Am I avoiding certain kinds of service out of inertia or repulsion?

16. Do I pity those in need?

17. Am I sacrificing my physical or emotional health in order to serve?

18. Do I have feelings of guilt, discontent, worries, or embarrassment when I serve?

19. Do I have awkward moments of nervous laughter or flashes of irritability or anger when I serve?

20. Do I serve those outside my home with greater respect and compassion than I exhibit toward my own family?

EXPLORING EMOTIONAL REACTIONS

Whenever we react instead of respond to an interaction or situation, we have an opportunity to examine the shadow. We can choose to perceive our reactions as opportunities to increase our awareness.

Exercises for Exploring Emotional Reactions

Select one interaction or event in your life that involves giving or receiving service and that brings forth a strong positive or negative emotional reaction. Using the suggestions in this section, work with that event until you feel you have a basic understanding of your shadow tendencies.

1. Observe any all-or-none thinking. Note your use of either/or, black/white thinking and your use of all-inclusive words like never, always, and absolutely.

2. Write a paragraph or two about your feelings and your interpretation of the event. Substitute "I," "me," and "my" for all references to you, your, them, their, and they, and for peoples' proper names. Ask yourself if these qualities or traits are also true for you and if you want to deny that they might be.

3. Draw a seesaw. On one side of the seesaw, put all the words that describe your feelings and observations about the event or interaction. Put the opposite of each feeling and observation on the other side of the seesaw. Note which qualities or traits are true for you. Note if you want to deny that they might be.

4. Draw a large rectangle to represent a blackboard. Draw a line down the middle of the board. Select a person with whom you find fault. On the left-hand side list the faults you perceive in this person. On the right-hand side write the opposites of each fault. For example, if you have written "arrogance" as a fault, you would write "humility" as its opposite. Ask yourself which polarities you readily see in yourself and which ones you deny in yourself.

This above all: to thine own self be true, And it must follow, as the night the day, Thou canst not then be false to any man.

–WILLIAM SHAKESPEARE

Hidden Motivations Exercise [4]

Recall a helping situation in which the person you were helping became upset, resistant, or withdrew from you. Explore possible hidden motivations for service by responding to the following:

1. Describe the details of the situation from your point of view, delineating your motivations.

2. Describe the situation from the point of view of the other.

3. What emotional needs were you trying to meet through this relationship?

4. What did you actually receive?

5. Did this situation have an affect on your attitude about giving? If "yes," how so?

MONITORING CARE OF SELF

Attending to one's own physical, mental, emotional, and spiritual well-being is one of the greatest challenges of service. Failure to be vigilant of your needs will lead to neglect of your health. This neglect can result in mental and physical exhaustion, conflicted relationships, and loss of enthusiasm for life and service. Regularly engage your Witness Self to observe the times you forget to care for yourself. Set aside feelings of guilt or shame for not having noticed your needs or attended to your care.

Neglect Checklist

Place your awareness in your Witness Self in order to do this exercise without feelings of guilt or shame.

[4] Adapted from an exercise written by Kathleen Sheil.

As human beings, we are endowed with choice, and we cannot shuffle off our responsibility upon the shoulders of God or nature. We must shoulder it ourselves. It is up to us.

—ARNOLD TOYNBEE

On a blank sheet of paper make three columns, one titled Physical, another Mental/Emotional, another Spiritual. Under each title, list what you feel are ways you neglect that part of yourself when you are in service. You may list these ways in general or you may refer to a specific situation in which you gave or received service. Observe your areas of neglect. Attempt to be as complete and specific with your lists as possible.

METHODS FOR WORKING WITH THE SHADOW OF SERVICE

After you have identified your shadow tendencies, select one of the exercises from this section to begin working with your shadow. *Allow sufficient time to integrate your new learning and growth before you select and work with another situation.*

Communication in the form of dialogue is the most helpful tool for owning and integrating those parts of ourselves that we have disowned. As the two opposing parts of ourselves converse with one another, the hidden wisdom, the gold within the shadow, reveals itself. Rather than being in opposition, the energies of these opposing views paradoxically balance one another. Now we have a broader view of possibilities and can make a choice appropriate to the situation.

We waste energy when we oppose life's problems and events rather than view them paradoxically. As Robert Johnson wrote, to "transform opposition into paradox is to allow both sides of an issue to exist in equal dignity and worth....Two opposing wishes will cancel each other if I let them remain in opposition. But if I sit with them awhile they will fashion a solution that is agreeable to both; or even better, a situation that is superior to either one."

Allow sufficient time to integrate your new learning and growth before you select and work with another situation.

Polarity Dialogue

As the two opposing parts of ourselves converse with one another, the hidden wisdom, the gold within the shadow, reveals itself.

A dialogue is a conversation. As a healing tool in shadow work, dialoguing allows you to converse with those parts of yourself you have rejected. You can dialogue by visualizing the quality or by writing to it and then writing its response to you. Dialoguing provides an opportunity to express your thoughts and feelings. As importantly, it allows an opportunity to listen to the other's point of view. Before beginning a dialogue, center for a few minutes, engage your Witness Self, and affirm your intention to communicate with clarity and honest.

Select a quality whose polarity you would like to integrate. Dialoguing with polarities of your shadow can be done in one or more of the following ways:

1. Verbalize or write a dialogue/conversation between tow opposing qualities. Allow each quality to express its feelings, unfulfilled needs, and desire to defend itself. The purpose of the conversation is to allow each polarity to be heard and to communicate its point of view. If the conversation deteriorates into a defensive right/wrong dialogue, re-center, engage your Witness Self, and begin the dialogue anew.

2. Verbalize or write a dialogue between the True Self and each of the opposite parts. Ask if each has any fears. Ask each about needs unfulfilled. Ask about rewards for identifying with each polarity. Reassure and comfort each quality. If you step out of your True Self, re-center, engage your Witness Self, and begin the dialogue anew.

3. Draw a seesaw, drawing yourself standing on its fulcrum. With your awareness of standing on the fulcrum, observe each polarity with openness to learning its wisdom. Then ask what each side wants to say. Listen to each side with total presence and respect.

Be open to nonjudgementally hearing both viewpoints. Do not take sides or view one as right and one as wrong. If you find yourself taking sides, re-center yourself, engaged your Witness Self, and resume the dialogue.

4. Place two chairs opposing one another. In your mind, center, engage your Witness Self, and place your awareness on the fulcrum of the seesaw. Follow these steps:

- Sit in one chair and project the disowned part out in front of you onto the opposing chair. Notice what it looks like physically. Observe the quality of its nonverbal and emotional expressions.

- Ask it who it is and what it needs from you.

- Get up and sit in the opposing chair. Verbally respond from the disowned part.

- Switch chairs, thanking this part for what it has said. Ask how it helped you when you were young. Ask how it helps you now.

- Switch chairs and allow the disowned part to respond.

- Switch chairs and assure the disowned part you have heard what it has said. Express appreciation for the part's willingness to talk with you.

5. Examine ways you might be denying parts of yourself and projecting these parts onto the situation or the person you are serving by following these steps: [5]

a. Describe the event or interaction of service in which you have reacted with an emotional upset.

b. What are your feelings, interests, and needs around the upset?

c. Who or what from your past does the theme of the event

If you look for the truth outside yourself, it gets farther and farther away.

–TUNG-SHAN

---

[5] Adapted from Charles Whitfield, *Boundaries and Relationships*, pp. 96-99.

or interaction remind you? When was it and how old were you? What happened?

d. What painful aspect of yourself might you be projecting onto the present situation or interaction?

e. What underlying attitudes or outmoded beliefs might be operating?

f. What is the message of the conflict?

g. How have you been in this conflict before from the other side, the other point of view?

Mandorla Drawing

The symbol of a mandorla is two circles overlapping, with each circle representing the competing demands of heaven and earth and the overlapping part representing the reconciliation of opposites. Draw a mandorla, placing symbols representing the opposing quality on each side. Center and engage your Witness Self. Then draw a possible reconciliation symbol in the overlapping part. Contemplate your drawing and what truth about your shadow it might be revealing.

For example, if you are working with the polarities of acceptance and rejection of your service, you might draw a symbol of arms open for acceptance and arms closed for rejection. When contemplating a symbol for the overlapping circles, you might draw two hands clasped. Another symbol of acceptance might be an open door, rejection might be a closed door. The overlapping circle might be a place in nature, such as a meadow. The symbols you draw will reflect the emotional reconciliation of the polarities of service unique to you.

If you have built castles in the air, your work need not be lost; that is where they should be. Now put foundations under them.

–Henry David
Thoreau

Mountain Visualization [6]

Sit in a comfortable position and close your eyes. Center. Engage the Witness Self. Acknowledge the spaciousness of your essence.

Select a shadow quality of your service that you choose to transform. Personify this quality in some way. What does it look like? An animal? An insect? A person? What are its features?

Stand face to face with this quality. Be patient; have courage. Stay with the process. Re-center if necessary. Engage the Witness Self.

As you face this part of yourself, ask what message it has for you. What does it want to say to you? Take a few minutes and talk with it; listen to its message.

Now, image the two of you transported to a most beautiful valley. The two of you find yourselves among grass, trees, flowers; you see the mountain. You feel safe in this place.

The two of you begin to walk up the mountain together, side by side. Walk slowly; take your time. If you can do so, hold the hand of your quality or hold your quality in some way. If you cannot seem to do this, allow your quality to walk or move in some way alongside you, as you both ascend the mountain.

You notice as you ascend that the air is becoming purer and purer and you welcome the silence of the heights and beautiful scenery. Re- main aware of the presence of your personified shadow quality beside you.

As the two of you climb, you begin to notice that the quality is slowly changing; it's becoming something else. It is gradually transforming; it may even totally transform.

You reach the top of the mountain and the sun shines down on the two of you. And now you may still see yet another

God is always using the stranger to introduce us to the strangeness of truth. To be inhospitable to strangers or strange ideas, however unsettling they may be, is to be hostile to the possibility of truth.

—PARKER PALMER

[6] Adapted from Piero Ferrucci, *What We May Be*, pp. 56-57.

transformation of your quality. What has the shadow quality become? Let it express its constructive side, its highest potential.

Slowly open your eyes and ask yourself these questions. What did I experience? What transformations occurred and what might this tell me about my service? Did a transformation not occur or did I want to resist following the imagery?

It is for us to pray not for tasks equal to our powers, but for powers equal to our tasks, to go forward with a great desire forever beating at the door of our hearts as we travel towards our distant goal.

—HELEN KELLER

If you did not experience a transformation of your shadow quality, you may need to do the exercise again. You need to allow it to be what it is in order for it to communicate with you and transform into its highest potential. If you negatively judge the shadow quality or do not accept it as part of yourself, its constructive side will not appear. The quality then may increase in intensity and move back into the unconscious.

Recapitulation Practice

The recapitulation exercise brings to your awareness positive and negative thoughts and feelings you have failed to acknowledge in your day's experiences. By observing and acknowledging your shadow tendencies of the day, you balance your conscious and unconscious energies. You will also have a more peaceful sleep and are apt to awaken the next morning with greater enthusiasm and vitality.

Just before falling asleep, do one of the Centering Exercises. Then, briefly review the events of the day from night back to morning. Review these events in the broad context of giving and receiving service.

Acknowledge any feelings that arise about these events. Ask yourself if you might have projected any of your shadow material into these interactions or if you have in any way avoided giving or receiving. Ask whether you have neglected your physical, emotional, mental, or spiritual well-being in any interaction during the day. Expand your awareness around the situations and acknowledge any projections, denials, or areas of neglect.

Complete the recapitulation exercise by acknowledging your willingness to review the day in this way. Also acknowledge the day for its gift of opportunities for learning and growth. Follow your acknowledgments with a centering or witnessing exercise.

Reframing Exercise

Select a situation involving service in which you were aware of either blaming and finding-fault or idolizing. Write a brief description of the situation.

Now, close your eyes and relieve the events, focusing on what was said and done and what your feelings and thoughts were at the time. Open your eyes and journal what seemed most important to you about this situation.

Close your eyes, again reliving the situation. Focus on acknowledging what you might be projecting, denying, or neglecting. Open your eyes and write down your awarenesses.

Close your eyes. Ask yourself how you would like to respond if this kind of situation or interaction were to happen again. Write down your intention.

Close your eyes. Relive the situation, carrying out your intention. Once complete, acknowledge your willingness to learn and grow and journal any awareness or insights.

Never vaunt your gifts to the poor or expect their gratitude, but rather be grateful to them for giving you the occasion of practicing charity to them.

–SWAMI VIVEKANANDA

*A*PPRECIATION

To Peggy Tabor Millin, an author in her own right, who believed in the message of *Born to Serve* and who joined me in serving the book as an altar of devotion. The integrity of our writer-editor partnership allowed me to engage wholeheartedly in the rigorous discipline of writing. Together, we experienced the depth of the book's teaching—that service, as life, is indeed a masterpiece of the soul.

*A*CKNOWLEDGMENTS

Born to Serve is the fruit of actions made on my behalf by many people, beginning with Mrs. Schnegas, an intuitively gifted midwife who with a spirit of True Service tended to my critical needs as a newborn.

Throughout my life, I have been blessed with teachers and professors who believed in my potential when I did not. I am especially indebted to principal Melvin Taylor, and to professors and staff at Ball State, Stanford, and Northwestern universities. Without the steadfast encouragement of these individuals, my life truly would not be what it is today.

I am appreciative for the years of work experience in community service agencies and universities in Alaska, Illinois, and California. I am especially grateful to the staff and children at the Alaska Children's Treatment Center in Anchorage and my colleagues and graduate students at the Department of Learning Disabilities, University of the Pacific at Pacific Medical Center in San Francisco.

In 1980, when I joined the Institute for Attitudinal Studies, I felt inspired to explore the depth and breadth of the relationship of personal growth to service. I am grateful to Judith Skutch Whitson, Molly Whitehouse, Shirley Fine, and Jean and Merrill Whitman for supporting me during the initial years of this critical stage of my soul's journey.

Many facilitators and volunteers at the Institute have supported the writing of this book. I am especially thankful for the contributions of Liz Cooper, David Knepper, Nellie Lauth, Jane McNew, Carolyn Riesenman, Kathleen Sheil, Dena Sollins Verrill, Grace Spring, and Karen Watt. I also thank Kay Adair and the 300 people who completed the initial service questionnaire, which served to help me clarify the purpose and content of the book. I thank the book's critical readers: Martha Brumbaugh, Wayne Caskey, Shirley Fine, Barbara Fornoff, Milyn Jordan, Bill Mahoney, Jon McBride, Lou Millin, Judith Perry, Julia Preston, Kathleen Sheil, Carolyn Wallace, Karen Watt, Cynthia Williams, and Merrill Whitman.

Several spiritual teachers have shared their insights about service by example or through letters and interviews. I am grateful to Roberto Assagioli, Swami Chidvalasananda, His Holiness The Dalai Lama, Kempo Konchog Gyaltshen, the teacher Michael, Shrikrishna Kashyap, Bhakti Tirtha Swami Krsnapada, and Stephen Levine.

Pervading the spirit of *Born to Serve* is the contribution my family has made toward my understanding of service. I acknowledge my parents, George and Ruth Struve, my brother, John and his family, and my sisters, Mary Martin and Betty Werner and their families. I will always appreciate my early life in Kouts, Indiana, as it was in this small country town that I began my lifelong quest to understand service.

ℬIBLIOGRAPHY

Almaas, A. H. *Luminous Night's Journey*. Berkeley, Calif: Diamond Books, 1995.

———. *The Void: Inner Spaciousness and Ego Structure*. Berkeley, Calif.: Diamond Books, 1992.

Armstrong, Regis J., and Ignatius C. Brady, trans. *Francis and Clare: The Complete Works*. New York: Paulist Press, 1982.

Ashrama, Advaita. *Great Women of India*. Calcutta: Sun Lithographing Co., 1982.

Assagioli, Roberto. *The Act of Will*. New York: Penguin Books, 1982.

Bailey, Alice A., and Djwhal Khul. *The Soul: The Quality of Life*. New York: Lucis Publishing Company, 1974.

———. *Ponder on This*. New York: Lucis Publishing Co., 1971.

———. *Serving Humanity*. New York: Lucis Publishing Co., 1972.

Birnbaum, Philip, trans. *Mishneh Torah: Maimonides' Code of Law and Ethics*. Brooklyn, N. Y.: Hebrew Publishing Co., 1944.

Brandon, David. *Zen in the Art of Helping*. London: Routledge & Kegan Paul, 1976.

Caldicott, Helen. *A Desperate Passion*. New York: W. W. Norton & Co., 1996.

Carlson, Richard, and Benjamin Shield, eds. *Healers on Healing*. Los Angeles: Jeremy P. Tarcher, Inc., 1989.

Chodron, Pema. *The Wisdom of No Escape and the Path of Loving-Kindness*. Boston: Shambhala Publications, 1991.

Chodron, Thubten. *Open Heart, Clear Mind*. Ithaca, N. Y.: Snow Lion Publications, 1990.

Colby, Ann. *Some Do Care: Contemporary Lives of Moral Commitment*. New York: Maxwell Macmillan International, 1992.

Coles, Robert. *The Call of Service*. Boston: Houghton Mifflin Co., 1993.

Dalai Lama. *Essential Teachings*. Translated by Zelie Pollon. Berkeley, Calif.: North Atlantic Books, 1994.

———. *Kindness, Clarity, and Insight*. Translated and edited by Jeffrey Hopkins, co-edited by Elizabeth Napper. Ithaca, N. Y.: Snow Lion Publications, 1984.

Dass, Ram, and Mirabai Bush. *Compassion in Action: Setting Out on the Path of Service*. New York: Bell Tower, 1992.

Dass, Ram, and Paul Gorman. *How Can I Help?: Stories and Reflections on Service*. New York: Alfred A. Knopf, 1985.

Diamant, Anita, with Howard Cooper. *Living A Jewish Life: Jewish Traditions, Customs and Values for Today's Families*. New York: HarperCollins, 1991.

Easwaran, Eknath. *The End of Sorrow*. The *Bhagavad Gita* for Daily Living, vol. 1. Petaluma, Calif.: Nilgiri Press, n.d.

Ferrucci, Piero. *What We May Be: Techniques for Psychological and Spiritual Growth Through Psychosynthesis*. New York: G. P. Putnam's Sons, 1982.

Fowler, James W. *Stages of Faith: The Psychology of Human Development and the Quest for Meaning*. New York: HarperCollins, 1981.

Fortune, Dion. *The Mystical Qabalah*. York Beach, Mass.: Samuel Weiser, Inc., 1984.

French, R. M., trans. *The Way of a Pilgrim*. San Francisco: HarperCollins, 1973.

Fritz, Robert. *The Path of Least Resistance: Learning to Become the Creative Force in Your Own Life*. New York: Fawcett Columbine, 1989.

Fuller, Millard. *The Theology of the Hammer*. Macon, Ga.: Smyth & Helwys Publishing, Inc., 1994.

Gaillard, Frye. *If I Were a Carpenter: Twenty Years of Habitat for Humanity*. Winston-Salem, N. C.: John F. Blair, Publisher, 1996.

Goddard, Dwight, ed. *A Buddhist Bible*. Boston: Beacon Press, 1938.

Gordon, Sol. *Is There Anything I Can Do?: Helping a Friend When Times Are Tough*. New York: Delaconte Press, 1994.

Groeschel, Benedict J. *Spiritual Passages: The Psychology of Spiritual Development "for Those Who Seek."* New York: Crossroads, 1992.

Greaves, Helen. *Testimony of Light*. Essex, England: Neville Spearman Publishers, 1969.

Haich, Elisabeth. *Initiation*. Palo Alto, Calif.: Seed Center, 1974.

Hahn, Thich Nhat. *Being Peace*. Berkeley, Calif.: Parallax Press, 1987.

Harding, M. Esther. *The "I" and the "Not-I": A Study in the Development of Consciousness*. Princeton, N. J.: Princeton University Press, 1965.

———. *Psychic Energy: Its Source and Its Transformation*. New York: Bollingen Foundation, 1973.

Helminski, Kabir Edmund. *Living Presence: A Sufi Way to Mindfulness and the Essential Self*. New York: G. P. Putnam's Sons, 1992.

Hollender, Jeffrey A. *How to Make the World a Better Place: A Guide to Doing Good*. New York: Morrow, 1990.

Hinnells, John R., ed. *A Handbook of Living Religions*. New York: Penguin Books, 1984.

Hoodwin, Shepherd. *The Journey of Your Soul: A Channel Explores Channeling and the Michael Teachings*. New York: Summerjoy Press, 1995.

Hoose, Phillip M. *It's Our World, Too!: Stories of Young People Who Are Making a Difference*. Boston: Joy Street Books, 1993.

Ingram, Catherine. *In the Footsteps of Gandhi: Conversations with Spiritual Social Activists*. Berkeley, Calif.: Parallax Press, 1990.

Johnson, Robert A. *Owning Your Own Shadow: Understanding the Dark Side of the Psyche*. New York: HarperCollins. 1993.

Jung, C. G. *Synchronicity: An Acausal Connecting Principle*. Translated by R. F. C. Hull. Princeton, N. J.: Princeton University Press, 1973.

Kilpatrick, Joseph, and Sanford Danziger. *Better Than Money Can Buy: The New Volunteers*. Winston-Salem, N. C.: Innersearch Publishing, 1996.

Kohn, Alfie. *The Brighter Side of Human Nature: Altruism and Empathy in Everyday Life*. New York: Basic Books, 1990.

Kornfield, Jack. *A Path with Heart: A Guide through the Perils and Promises of Spiritual Life*. New York: Bantam Books, 1993.

Levine, Stephen. *Healing into Life and Death*. New York: Doubleday, 1987.

———. *Who Dies?: An Investigation of Conscious Living and Conscious Dying*. Garden City, N. Y.: Anchor Books, 1982.

Lincoln, Victoria. *Teresa: A Woman. A Biography of Teresa of Avila*. Albany, N.Y.: State University of New York Press, 1984.

Lukas, Mary, and Ellen Lukas. *Teilhard*. New York: McGraw-Hill Book Company, 1981.

Luks, Allan. *The Healing Power of Doing Good: The Health and Spiritual Benefits of Helping Others*. New York: Fawcett Colombine, 1992.

McBee, Shar. *To Lead Is to Serve: How to Attract Volunteers and Keep Them*. Honolulu: Shar McBee, 1994.

Meek, George W. *Healers and the Healing Process*. Wheaton, Ill.: Theosophical Publishing House, 1977.

Meltzer, Milton. *Who Cares? Millions Do: A Book About Altruism*. New York: Walker, 1994.

Moore, Thomas. *Care of the Soul: A Guide for Cultivating Depth and Sacredness in Everyday Life*. New York: HarperCollins, 1992.

Muktananda, Swami. *From the Finite to the Infinite*. Vol. 1. South Fallsburg, N. Y.: SYDA Foundation, 1989.

O'Brien, Justin. *Christianity and Yoga: A Meeting of Mystic Paths*. London: Penguin Group, 1989.

Oughton, Jerrie. *The Magic Weaver of Rugs: A Tale of the Navajo*. Boston: Houghton Mifflin Company, 1994.

Perlman, Helen H. *Relationship, the Heart of Helping People*. Chicago: University of Chicago Press, 1979.

Prabhavananda, Swami. *The Spiritual Heritage of India*. Hollywood, Calif.: Vedanta Press, 1963.

Prabhupada, Swami, A. C. *The Nectar of Devotion: The Complete Science of Bhakti-Yoga*. Los Angeles: Bhaktivedanta Book Trust, 1970.

Prejean, Helen. *Dead Man Walking*. New York: Vintage Books,1993.

Phillips, Donald T. *Lincoln On Leadership: Executive Strategies for Tough Times*. New York: Warner Books, 1992.

Renard, John. *Seven Doors to Islam: Spirituality and the Religious Life of Muslims*. Berkeley, Calif.: University of California Press, 1996.

Rinpoche, Guru. *The Tibetan Book of the Dead: The Great Liberation Through Healing the Bardo*. Boulder, Colo.: Shambhala Publications, Inc., 1975.

Rinpoche, Sogyal. *The Tibetan Book of Living and Dying*. San Francisco: Harper, 1992.

Sanford, John A. *Soul Journey: A Jungian Analyst Looks at Reincarnation*. New York: Crossroad Publishing Company, 1991.

Senge, Peter. *The Fifth Discipline: The Art and Practice of the Learning Organization*. New York: Doubleday/Currency, 1990.

Senge, Peter. *The Fifth Discipline Fieldbook: Strategies and Tools for Building Learning Organizations*. New York: Currency, Doubleday, 1994.

Sinetar, Marsha. *Ordinary People as Monks and Mystics: Lifestyles for Self-Discovery*. New York: Paulist Press, 1986.

Small, Jacqueline. *Becoming Naturally Therapeutic: A Return to the True Essence of*

Helping. New York: Bantam Books, 1990.

Spaide, Deborah. *Teaching Your Child to Care: How to Discover and Develop the Spirit of Charity in Your Children.* Seaucus, N. J.: Carol Publishing, 1995.

Stewart, Judy-Carol. *Reiki Touch: The Essential Handbook.* Atlanta, Ga.: New Leaf Distributing Company, 1995.

Taylor, Kylea. *The Ethics of Caring: Honoring the Web of Life in Our Professional Healing Relationships.* Santa Cruz, Calif.: Hanford Mead Publishers, 1985.

Teresa, Mother. *A Simple Path.* New York: Ballantine Books, 1995.

Teresa of Avila, Saint. *Interior Castle.* Translated by E. Allison Peers. New York: Doubleday, 1989.

The Way to the Kingdom. Marina del Rey, Calif.: DeVorss & Company, 1978.

Tillard, Francoise. *Fanny Mendelssohn.* Portland, Oreg.: Amadeus Press, 1992.

Trout, Susan S. *To See Differently.* Alexandria, Va.: Three Roses Press, 1990.

Underhill, Evelyn. *The Ways of the Spirit.* Edited and with an introduction by Grace Adolphsen Brame. New York: The Crossroad Publishing Company, 1994.

Vivekananda, Swami. *Education.* Mylapore, Madras: Sri Ramakrishna Math, 1994.

Wallop, Douglass. *Damn Yankees.* New York: W. W. Norton, 1954.

Weiss, Brian L. *Many Lives, Many Masters.* New York: Simon & Schuster Inc., 1988.

Whitfield, Charles. *Boundaries and Relationships: Knowing, Protecting, and Enjoying the Self.* Deerfield Beach, Fla.: Health Communications, Inc., 1993.

Wilber, Ken. *A Brief History of Everything.* Boston: Shambhala, 1996.

———. *The Spectrum of Consciousness.* Wheaton, Ill.: The Theosophical Publishing House, 1977.

Wilson, Marlene. *You Can Make a Difference: Helping Others and Yourself through Volunteering.* Boulder, Colo.: Volunteer Management Associates, 1990.

Wuthnow, Robert. *Sharing the Journey: Support Groups and America's New Quest for Community.* New York: Simon & Schuster, Inc., 1994.

Yawkey, Thomas. *Caring: Activities to Teach Young Children to Care for Others.* Englewood Cliffs, N. J.: Prentice Hall, 1982.

Zimmerman, Richard. *What Can I Do to Make a Difference?: A Positive Action Sourcebook.* New York: Penguin Books, 1991.

Zohar, Danah, and Ian Marshall. *The Quantum Society: Mind, Physics, and a New Social Vision*. New York: William Morrow and Co., Inc., 1994.

Zweig, Connie, and Jeremiah Abrams, eds. *Meeting the Shadow: The Hidden Power of the Dark Side of Human Nature*. New York: G. P. Putnam's Sons, 1976.

$\mathcal{I}$NDEX

ABOUT THE AUTHOR

Susan S. Trout, Ph.D., is Executive Director of the Institute for Attitudinal Studies in Alexandria, Virginia. She coordinates and develops support and study programs, trains group leaders, leads workshops in personal growth, trains facilitators for those having physical emotional or spiritual health needs, and develops research projects in mind-body-spirit disciplines.

In service organizations in Alaska, Illinois, and California, Dr. Trout worked as a specialist and researcher in communication and neurological disorders. She spent fourteen years as a professor, chairperson, and researcher at the University of the Pacific and University of California Medical Centers in San Francisco. In 1980, she co-founded the Institute for Attitudinal Studies.

Dr. Trout holds graduate degrees from Stanford and Northwestern universities in psychoneurology, deaf education, audiology, speech pathology, and communication disorders. She has authored several professional articles and facilitator training manuals for adults and adolescents. She is also author of *To See Differently*, published by Three Roses Press in 1990.

ABOUT THE INSTITUTE FOR ATTITUDINAL STUDIES

Founded in 1980 as a volunteer, nonprofit, educational and non-sectarian spiritual organization, the Institute for Attitudinal Studies offers service, training, research and publishing programs dedicated to personal growth and community service within the philosophical framework of attitudinal studies. The core processes of attitudinal studies are personal growth, service, facilitation, communication, conflict resolution, leadership and organizational design. Contributing disciplines include psychosynthesis, the *enneagram*, depth psychology, dream psychology, attitudinal healing, death and dying, energy work, metaphysics, and Western and Eastern spiritual thought.

Support groups, facilitation and conflict resolution services, study groups, courses, and workshops are offered by the Institute that support the emotional and spiritual well-being of people of all ages in a wide variety of life circumstances.

Extensive training programs prepare adults and high schoool students to be facilitators and mediators and prepare group leaders to lead these trainings. Trainings for individuals and organizations are also offered in leadership, organizational design, team building, group process, and conflict resolution.

Research projects evaluate the effectiveness of the Institute's trainings, prepare materials on leadership and organizational models, and study the dynamics of the healing process and service. The Three Roses Press publishes the Institute's newsletter, books, manuals, and educational materials.

For more information, please contact: Institute for Attitudinal Studies
P.O. Box 19222 Alexandria, VA 22320 703-706-5333